TELEOLOGICAL EXPLANATIONS

TELEOLOGICAL EXPLANATIONS

An Etiological Analysis of Goals and Functions

Larry Wright

UNIVERSITY OF CALIFORNIA PRESS

Berkeley   Los Angeles   London

University of California Press
Berkeley and Los Angeles
University of California Press, Ltd.
London, England

ISBN: 0-520-03086-9
Library of Congress Catalog Card Number: 75-17284
Copyright © 1976 by The Regents of the University of California
Printed in the United States of America

FOR DAISY

CONTENTS

[vii]

ACKNOWLEDGMENTS

The research for this essay was supported by the National Science Foundation and by the Humanities Institute of the University of California. I am grateful for that support.

I would also like to thank the following for providing the quoted material in the text: *History and Theory, Philosophy of Science, Studies in the History and Philosophy of Science, The Philosophical Review,* Cambridge University Press, MacMillan & Co., Princeton University Press, Routledge and Kegan Paul, John Wiley and Sons.

L. W.

INTRODUCTION

The appeal to teleological principles of explanation within the body of natural science has had an unfortunate history. It has been unfortunate not because the appeals themselves were inappropriate but rather because in every case the *defense* of the teleological principle has at some stage become methodologically suspect. The zealous supporters of the teleological principle have almost universally attempted to shield their account from slings and arrows of the opposition in ways that have departed from the mainstream of scientific procedure. Whenever this sort of thing occurs, it tends to stigmatize a rejected theory as ridiculous and wrongheaded, not simply mistaken; the theory gets rejected as wrong *in principle*, not just in fact.

Of course, this fate has befallen a large number of non-teleological theories in the history of science too, for example, the transmutation of metals, the caloric theory of heat, phlogiston theory, ether theory, and the inheritance of acquired characteristics, to name only a few. The treatment of *these* theories by scientists and philosophers of science has also tended to raise issues of logic and method, to the exclusion of empirical considerations. But only *some* theories of this kind have been so completely rejected by science: other incarnations of mechanical explanatory principle obviously have survived. In the case of a discredited theory of the orthodox casual-mechanical sort, the object of ridicule could not be mechanical explanation simpliciter, because that principle was working

very well at the same level in other applications. So the
ridicule has focused on the *specific* mechanical notion
involved in each of these cases. *Phlogiston* came to be discredited, but not the notion of invisible substances
leaving or joining a sample during chemical reaction.
Caloric was abandoned, but not the notion of heat flow.

By contrast, *all* the famous appeals to teleological principle at a basic theoretical level in natural science apparently have met with this fate: early Greek animism, Aristotle's natural places, Paley's watchmaker, Driesche's
entelechy—all have been discredited in a way parallel to
phlogiston and ether. Each has left a distinct odor of rotten method. Hence it has been very easy for scientists and
philosophers to take the next step and raise logical and
methodological questions about the very notion of teleological explanation itself. Anything that has been so consistently and fundamentally wrong, and has caused such
ugly disputes among intelligent men must, it seemed, be
intrinsically obfuscatory.

Some have gone so far as to claim that the major product of the Galilean revolution, which has made possible
the great gains of modern science, is the insistence that
science forever reject its earlier dark dalliance with teleological conceptualizations: intellectual progress demands
we wash our hands of them.

The defense of this position usually appeals to general
trends or drifts within the whole of science, and, as an
argument for proscription, it is not the sort of thing philosophers will take very seriously in their more sober
moments. But philosophers (as opposed to scientists or
historians) who have concerned themselves with teleology
typically have been too cautious to urge the complete
elimination of teleological concepts from all objective discourse. Instead the influence of the 'general trends' argu-

ment has been largely to impose a flavor of post-Galilean mechanism on empiricist accounts of teleological notions; it has underwritten the view that hardheaded scientific objectivity requires us to characterize legitimate teleology in terms of underlying mechanical regularities. This in turn accounts, I think, for the enthusiasm of empiricist philosophers for radical conceptual surgery in this analytical enterprise. Their descriptions of 'all teleology comes to,'[1] or 'what functions statements actually claim,'[2] usually offer us a disemboweled teleological notion shorn even of its original outline. Often, by the author's own admission, the carcass is hardly worth saving.[3] As a consequence, empiricist caveats concerning the legitimate use of teleological concepts devolve largely to disclaimers such as 'functional analyses are not explanations,'[4] 'functions are not teleological,'[5] and 'teleological "explanations" do not explain anything' but rather represent a 'heuristic device.'[6]

Demonstrating that this radical reconstructionism and its accompanying stark warnings are mistaken and un-

1. See, for example, Ernest Nagel, *The Structure of Science* (New York: Harcourt, Brace and World, 1961), Chap. 12; R.B. Braithwaite, *Scientific Explanation* (Cambridge: Cambridge University Press, 1953), Chap. 10; and Morton Beckner, *The Biological Way of Thought* (Berkeley and Los Angeles: University of California Press, 1968), Chap. 7.

2. See, for example, Beckner, *Biological Way*, Chap. 6; John Canfield's article "Teleological Explanation in Biology," in *The British Journal for the Philosophy of Science*, vol. 14, no. 56, pp. 285-295; and Carl Hempel's article "The Logic of Functional Analysis," in L. Gross, ed., *Symposium on Sociological Theory* (New York: Harper and Row, 1959).

3. A clear example of this can be found in Hempel, "Logic of Functional Analysis," p. 287.

4. Beckner, *Biological Way*, p. 112.

5. This seems implicit in Ernest Nagel's discussion on p. 541 of his article "Teleological Explanations and Teleological Systems," in Feigl, H. & M. Brodbeck, eds., *Readings in the Philosophy of Science* (New York: Appleton-Century-Crofts, 1953), pp. 537-558.

6. C. Hempel and P. Oppenheim, "Studies in the Logic of Scientific Explanation," *Philosophy of Science* 15: 145.

helpful is, of course, a length task, and constitutes the major burden of the three following chapters. However, something definite can be said at this point about the perspective from which such analyses seem to flow; and this will set the tone for the argument that follows.

The tendency of scientists and philosophers to couch their criticism of a rejected theory in methodological rather than empirical terms is generally most unfortunate. This is both because doing so nearly always misrepresents the history of science, and, more importantly, because it offers to the philosophy of science an oversimplified caricature of scientific methodology. In virtually every case referred to above, teleological and non-teleological alike, the verdict of methodological monstrosity is brought against the theory at its worst, not at its best. It is the natural progress of a theory on its way to defeat and replacement that it be 'adjusted' in the face of adverse observations. And it is also quite natural, toward the end of that process, for the sanguine proponents of such a theory to lose sight of the rationale of the exercise and to continue adjusting long after the procedure has lost its point and plausibility. Accordingly, the later stages in the evolution of such a theory tend to drift durther and further from the norms of defensible scientific procedure. So if, as usually happens, we choose the last, or one of the last versions of a discredited theory to represent the competition faced by the succeeding theory, we have a ready-made strawman: knocking it down is both easy and misleading. It seems to fall of its own weight, with no help from the data: it is intrinsically flawed. Examining an early version of nearly any discredited natural scientific theory reveals a methodologically purer, if empirically less plausible, hypothesis. And since every explanatory principle can be abused, it is illegitimate to impugn a principle simply because its abuse has managed to find its way into the literature.

At least some responsibility for the general oversimplification of this important issue must be placed on the role Newtonian mechanics has played as a paradigm of physical theory: it has obscured the nature and legitimacy of theoretical elasticity vis-à-vis experimental investigation. It is standard scientific procedure for a theory to begin life as a rough-and-ready, partly metaphorical structuring of an area of study, and gradually take on clearer form as the *result* of empirical investigation. It is in a way cut to fit the phenomena. But at this early, inchoate stage such 'adjustments' are not to be disparaged as ad hoc (in the pejorative sense); rather, they are for the most part best characterized as 'discovering the properties of the entities postulated by the theory.' Although Newtonian mechanics has not been completely exempt from this procedure (e.g., one might argue that discovering the variation of inertial mass with relative velocity provided just such an adjustment), it is nevertheless an extreme case in this regard. Much more typical of workaday scientific theoretical progress are: chemical bonding theory, macrothermodynamical theory, the kinetic theory of matter, quantum mechanics and electrodynamics, the theory of light refraction, the elemental chemical theory embodied in the periodic table, Torricelli's barometric hypothesis, and even continental drift theory. In each of these cases, much of the initial effort was directed toward discovering the properties of the basic theoretical notions: for example, molecular bond, heat flow, microscopic particle of matter, electron shells and orbits, light rays, element, 'sea of air,' geological plate. But this activity can also be characterized as discovering the best way to flesh-out the initial, groping metaphors: 'bond,' 'flow,' 'parti-

cle,' 'shell,' 'orbit,' 'ray,' 'element,' 'sea,' 'plate.' Determining the point at which this process ceases to be discovery and becomes the blind, antiscientific defensiveness
of a theory in the throes of reluctant discomfiture is central to understanding the rationale of scientific theoretical progress. It is also very often difficult. Few theories
have the point demarcated as clearly as phlogiston theory
or ether theory, and even those cases require subtlety and
care for an accurate recounting.

In any case, it *is* clear that a presently discredited
explanatory principle could well have been given a less
defensive and more defensible construction than that
placed on it by its last, desperate defenders. It should not
be surprising that the history of science reveals the actual
existence of methodologically purer versions of these theories, which it does in virtually every case. But even after
establishing this general point, there is often a lingering
doubt about its applicability to teleological cases. What
would it be *like* to find a defensible formulation of a teleological theory? It is one thing to show that phlogiston
theory was a viable, wholly respectable theory of chemical
processes up to the moment it was 'adjusted' to accommodate the mercury calx experiment. It seems to be quite
another to discover that rocks have souls. Perhaps ether
theory *was* a perfectly legitimate approach to electromag-
netic propagation until it was modified in the face of the
Michelson-Morely result. But it might appear ludicrous
to compare that case to the theoretical development of
Driesch's entelechy. It is to this issue that we must now
turn. The primary argumentative burden of chapters two
and three will be to show in detail just what legitimate
teleological explanations look like; to accomplish that
will be the major conceptual object of this essay.

CHAPTER I

THE CHARGES AGAINST
TELEOLOGY

The antipathy toward teleological explanations and conceptualizations, which is felt by many philosophers, scientists, and historians, stems more or less directly from the
horror stories surrounding the deployment of these concepts in certain classic contexts. Arguments for vitalism,
panpsychism, and a divine creator have sometimes involved teleological conceptualizations in dubious or
openly fraudulent methodological practice and associated them with discredited scientific theories. This, of
course, is not sufficient to discredit the teleological concepts themselves, and most of those who have urged the
complete proscription of teleological concepts have been
sensitive to this point. But the arguments they produce
are usually more concerned to *avoid* the horror than to
locate it, even if something valuable is lost in the avoiding. It will be useful to examine some of these arguments
in order to note the common concerns of a variety of dis-
ciplinarians which must be taken seriously in this analytical enterprise.

In a discussion of Karl Marx's historical methodology,[1]
Kins Collins makes a rather long comment containing
several interesting contentions on teleology.

There are various generally accepted criteria of legitimacy that a
causal statement may not violate. One of them is that a cause not be

1. "Marx on the English Agricultural Revolution: Theory and Evidence," *History and Theory* (1967), p. 352 ff.

chronologically later than its effect. Hence, the assertion that history
moves towards a goal — *teleology* — is not legitimate. . . . Marx com-
bines teleological causes with legitimate ones, sometimes intimately,
as in the following representative case. According to Marx, society
requires that factory production expand, and since many more children than adults are needed as workers, the concomitant expansion
of the work force must take the form of a rapid turnover of generations. "Society's need is satisfied through early marriages, a necessary
consequence of the (indecent) living conditions the workers" are
forced to endure. Here we find a curious synchronization of a causal
chain working backwards through time from *society's need* with
another chain working forwards from the *worker's living conditions*.

Three further examples of teleology in Marx's view of English agri-
culture follow. (1) The growth of capitalism required that the yeo-
manry be annihilated, so it was, through the separation process.
(2) The capitalists in the cities (before 1750) aided the separation
process in order to turn land into a market commodity, extend the
area of large-scale farming, and increase their supply of workers.
(3) The capitalistic system required the peasants to be in a servile
condition, so they became so.

Karl Lowith has claimed: "What seems to be a scientific discovery
(i.e., Marxism) . . . is, on the contrary, from the first to the last sentence inspired by an eschatological faith," that is, by Marx's faith in
his goal, the classless society, "which, in its turn, 'determines' the
whole sweep and range of all particular statements." One need not
go so far as Lowith to admit that teleology plays a significant role in
Marx's system.

The following passage from a botany textbook makes
explicit some of the objections to teleological explanation
implicit in the quote from Kins Collins, and adds at least
one of its own.

A series of cause and effect relations such as this illustrates the
complexity of superficially simple plant responses and the dependence of an acceptable theory on the accumulation of a wide variety
of research data. Contrast this *cause and effect* explanation with

some of the *teleological* explanations of stomatal movement sometimes seen in print: that stomata open in the morning "so that the
plant can secure carbon dioxide for photosynthesis" and that stomata
close at night "in order to save water." Such teleological explanations, crediting the plant with intelligent and purposeful behavior,
are easy to formulate but totally inadequate in explaining plant
responses. Teleological explanations get the cart before the horse by
converting a possible result into a cause. If botanists were satisfied
with teleological explanations for plant behavior, research aimed at
discovery of the actual course of events would cease.[2]

One of the above themes occurs in an interestingly different form in a comment by B. F. Skinner on the nature
of behavioral science.

A spider does not possess the elaborate behavioral repertoire with
which it constructs a web because that web will enable it to capture
the food it needs to survive. It possesses this behavior because similar
behavior on the part of spiders in the past has enabled *them* to capture the food *they* needed to survive. A series of events have been relevant to the behavior of web-making in its earlier evolutionary history.
We are wrong in saying that we observe the purpose of the web when
we observe similar events in the life of the individual.[3]

These passages from a working historian, a pair of life
scientists, and a behavioral scientist raise a large number
of important issues and can be adequately discussed only
after a number of distinctions have been made. Fortunately, for our present purposes these issues and distinctions may be ignored: they will be raised and treated
at length in later chapters. For now our concern with
these passages may be limited to three allegations they
contain concerning the nature of teleological explana-

2. Victor A. Greulach and J. Edison Adams, *Plants: An Introduction to Modern Botany*, 2d ed., (New York: John Wiley & Sons, Inc., 1967), p. 261.
3. B.F. Skinner in David Braybrooke, *Philosophical Problems of the Social Scie- ences* (Sources in Philosophy) (New York: MacMillan, 1965), p. 52.

tions. These are, (*a*) that teleological explanations reverse the orthodox order of cause and effect, (*b*) that teleological explanations involve the illicit attribution of human mental characteristics to things other than human beings, and (*c*) that accepting teleological explanations would bring scientific research to a halt, at least in some fields. An explicit, detailed examination of these allegations will serve to introduce the argument of this essay.

EFFECTS AND CAUSES

The single outstanding feature common to all three of these passages is a concern over chronology. The time order of certain kinds of events is important to these authors, and a derangement of the proper event sequence is at least part of what they take teleological characterizations to be guilty of in the context of their discussions. Skinner's expression of the difficulty is perhaps more circumspect than the others, but it is hard to avoid the view that he is worried about precisely the same thing as Collins and the botanists: causes coming after their effects.

The reversal of cause and effect has long been hung like an albatross around the neck of teleology, but it is not clear how this view could have survived even modest scrutiny. No doubt there is implicit in the teleological appreciation of phenomena an essential forward-looking element. But there is nothing in any of the ordinary ascriptions of goals or functions or motives or purposes or aims or drives or needs or intentions which requires us to reverse the normal cause-before-effect sequence. When I explain my going to the store by saying I went 'in order to get some bread,' I do not imply that the actual act of purchase caused by going which preceded it. The purchase of bread was a *goal* of the action, not a cause. Perhaps my *having* of that particular goal could be viewed as a cause of the action; but that of course is something that preceded the action, and hence is not guilty of the egregious time-reversal imputed to teleological accounts of behavior.

Similarly, when we explain the rabbit's running as taking place 'in order to escape from the dog,' we never mean to say that the escape causes the running. Fright perhaps (and that, again, preceded the action) but not the escape itself: the escape is, once again, the *goal* of the behavior, not its cause. Exactly the same point can be made with respect to functional explanations. We might say, for example, that the circumferential grooves in pneumatic tire treads are there 'in order to prevent skids in wet weather.' But in saying so we certainly do not mean that the lack (or infrequency) of wet-weather skids is what produces the grooves. Ridges on the mold make the grooves in the tires; and this is perfectly compatible with the claim that the *function* of the grooves is to prevent skids when it rains. So also for stomata: 'in order to save water' proffers something as the *function* of their closing, and hence nothing that rivals the long, chemical analysis Gruelach and Adams mistakenly offer as an incompatible alternative account of stomatal behavior. To say that stomata close at night in order to save water is, of course, to offer some sort of explanation of why stomata close at night; and the major aim of this discourse will be to make as clear as possible just what sort of explanation this is. But we must begin by recognizing that what follows the 'in order to' in teleological explanations is not even offered as a simple cause, and that whatever sins against orthodoxy such explanations commit, reversing the usual order of cause and effect is not among them.

ANTHROPOMORPHISM

The worry, expressed by Greulach and Adams, that teleological explanation unavoidably invokes intelligence and conscious purpose, requires far more elaborate treatment. There is a sense in which this worry represents the central logical problem in a study of teleological concepts and their application. For if it is the case that teleological characterizations and explanations *do* necessarily rely upon the implicit appeal to conscious purpose, there then seems to be insuperable difficulty in the vast majority of their scientific and proto-scientific applications. What sponsors this worry?

It stems, I think, from the rather reasonable supposition that the paradigm case of teleological conceptualizations and explanation is of human, conscious, intentional behavior. These are the cases we feel most comfortable with, the cases from which the terminology seems naturally to spring, the cases we naturally invoke to explain what we mean by the teleological terms. If we concede this[4] we seem forced to say that to offer a teleological explanation in any *non*human case is to traffic in dubious metaphor: it's anthropomorphism isn't it? The word has a heavily pejorative ring; it seems merely to *name* the botanists worry.

Nevertheless, I think the worry is a great mistake. I think there is an important insight to be gained from regarding teleological accounts of nonhuman phenomena as metaphorical extensions of paradigmatically human concepts. But to think that this is necessarily a bad thing — to suppose that this counts against the objectivity

4. For the sake of this discussion I *will* concede this point. Doing so will serve to cover a number of analytical bets: it will graphically display the range of presuppositions from which the conclusion of this disquisition may be reached.

or value of teleological conceptualizations in such contexts — to suppose this unfits them for scientific deployment — is simply to misunderstand the notion of a metaphor.

Metaphors are sometimes disparaged as irredeemably unscientific, anathema to hardheaded scientific method. But it is not clear why this should be so. Of course it is possible to get into conceptual difficulty by reckless use of metaphor; but this does not differentiate metaphors from expressions used literally, as the history of philosophy eloquently testifies. So this possibility cannot support a general disparagement; it cannot rule metaphors out of science. And it seems to me that the negative aspect of the use of metaphors in science, and in exposition generally, has been overemphasized. A good metaphor, cautiously used, can be of irreplaceable value in many contexts in which scientists and laymen constantly find themselves. It is neither accident nor affliction that we use them so much. But this is contentious, as well as central to the argument of this essay; so it is important that the nature, value, and dangers of this fascinating device be made clear.

Expressions, or sets of expressions which have originated and developed their logical nuance in one context and by reference to a limited subject matter, will sometimes be metaphorically extended to other contexts and referents. If done with care and logical sensitivity, this process is unobjectionable and frequently fertile of insight. We speak of showers of shooting stars, and the cruel sea; we say of someone that he is a round peg in a square hole, and argue about whether the moon is dead. We speak this way not just for the poetry of it, but for insightful appreciation as well; and in doing so we virtually never seriously mislead the experienced language user.

To understand the role of metaphor in objective, exposistory prose, it is best to view it as perceptual aid. Wittgenstein is famous for pointing out the logical complexity—and potential difficulty—of 'drawing someone's attention to an aspect or characteristic of something,' especially something that has several *geometrically* indistinguishable characteristics. Distinguishing between the color and shape of a pencil is importantly similar to distinguishing between the grayness and sullenness of the sky. Metaphorical extension is one of the tools language users employ to make this logically subtle move. We are able metaphorically to draw attention to a complex or subtle characteristic of something by using terminology paradigmatically appropriate only to some *other* thing with which we are more, or differently, familiar. When we refer to a rebuff as 'stinging,' to a bit of prose as 'opague,' or to the silence as 'stunning,' we are picking out a specific feature or aspect of those things that would be much more difficult, perhaps wholly beyond our competence to do in any other way. It is simply a mistake to think of these metaphorical characterizations as irretrievably visceral or merely poetic; there are circumstances in which they are clearly appropriate, and others in which they are clearly not, and they are subject to arguments and tests of exactly the same kind as the more usual perceptual characterizations and the more usual perceptual aids.

Just as it is objectively demonstrable that eyeglasses aid the perceptions of the myopic, and hearing aids help the deaf, it is often unmistakably clear that a metaphor will be of perceptual value in a certain context. Quite ordinary reliability and intersubjectivity tests apply. There are circumstances in which characterizing a rebuff as 'stinging' *unquestionably* helps us understand (explain) the subsequent behavior of the one rebuffed. Sometimes, viewing traffic signals as 'fresh' or 'stale,' as opposed to merely red, green, and yellow, makes an *obvious* contribution to one's grasp of city driving. Characterizing a musical technique as 'cascading violins' quite objectively helps in its identification: often it can be picked out under that description by someone who has never heard it before.

Just as we can test whether Uncle Ned has his hearing aid turned up, or whether Sis needs a new pair of glasses, we can test whether someone *really* grasps the significance of a metaphor. We can determine whether his understanding or perceptual acuity has been enhanced in the requisite way. We can probe the understanding and exercise the acuity. "Which of the following cases would you characterize as being a round peg in a square hole?" "In such-and-such circumstances, would you describe the signal as fresh or stale, or perhaps, something in between?" "Which of the following is cascading violins, and in what way do the others depart from that characterization?" The ability to gain intersubjective agreement on tests like this is all the objective significance of a metaphorical insight requires. And in this it is an exact parallel of our color concepts: intersubjective identificatory agreement is all there is to the objectivity of our chromatic vocabulary.

Like the more orthodox perceptual aids, metaphors can be good, bad, or pernicious depending on whether they clarify, obscure, or delude. The obscurity and delusion have, of course, the same source as the insight: dragging familiar associations into novel contexts. It is sometimes not clear which of the inferences licensed by the paradigmatic application of a term are justifiably drawn from the application of that term in a specific instance of metaphorical extension. Virtually any remotely plausible metaphor will permit some of the ordinary inferences; and this is the mechanism of insight. But since a metaphor is by definition not a standard, literal application of the term in question, it follows logically that some of the inferences ordinarily implicit in the application of the term are vitiated by the extraordinary context. The value and danger of a metaphor in exposition is crucially dependent upon the ease with which we can distinguish the inferences it licenses from those it does not. Good metaphors are those which (for ordinary mortals, in the proper context) naturally pick out just the appropriate aspect or aspects, and drop the other (irrelevant or misleading) associations of the term's standard use. And there are innumerable illustrations in which this is just what happens. We do not expect to get wet standing under a shower of shooting stars, nor do we expect any rotten stench to emanate from a geologically dead moon; although in each of these cases *other* characteristics of the paradigm *do* transfer and organize our apprehension of the phenomenon. Indeed, the obviousness of the disanalogy will often make it almost impossible to run afoul of it, leaving the way clear for the more subtle characteristics that metaphors are primarily used to display: anyone caught tasting a traffic light to see if it was stale would be either joking or deranged. And no one objects that some round pegs in square holes are not perfectly cylindrical.

The examples discussed so far, however, represent a peculiarly unproblematic subset of metaphorical extensions. Political oratory is filled with the more problematic variety. We are told of puppets and dominoes in Southeast Asia. There is the sickness of societies and the silence of the American majority. In other areas we hear of hot

and cold media and warped space. The difference between merely bad metaphors and pernicious ones is that
in the former case it is simply not clear which inferences
(associations) are supposed to be licensed (underwritten)
in the extended application, whereas in the latter case the
implication is clear but illegitimate. In many contexts
(although perhaps not all) in which it is done, referring to
one of the mass media as 'hot' is simply confusing,
because it is not clear from the context whether we can
infer sweaty and oppressive, or, perhaps, erotic. Conversely, characterizing a simultaneous troop withdrawal
and bombing escalation as 'winding down' a war is just
pernicious: it quite explicitly tempts us to unjustified
inferences.

The enormous complexity of human perceptual skills
makes it very difficult to say anything both interesting
and completely general about the characteristics that
group metaphors into 'good,' 'bad,' and 'pernicious.' An
absolutely central disanalogy between paradigm and
extended use, as we have seen, does not even make it
likely that unlicensed inferences will be tempting. In general, the best that can be said is that if a certain point
cannot be made as conveniently or as well in literal terminology (literal exposition can be perniciously misleading
too, of course!), then the quality of a metaphor devolves
to the following utility calculation: by how much does the
value of the insight afforded by the metaphor exceed the
cost (difficulty) of taking sufficient care to avoid
unlicensed inferences. Of course, both the value and the
difficulty depend upon contingent facts about human
perception (just like the grinding of eyeglasses), but that
does not impugn the objectivity of the distinction. In
many circumstances they are clear, and their difference is
great enough that an objective determination can be

made. In practice, good, objective, descriptive metaphors are often simple to identify. In most contexts there is simply no problem with the descriptive force of 'green recruit,' 'explosive temper,' 'new plateau,' 'tip of the iceberg.' These are just as intersubjective as 'green grass' and 'noisy corridor.'

It has been forcefully argued, however, that there is a *formal* requirement that legitimate expository metaphor must meet: it must be capable of literal paraphrase or translation. The claim that the moon is dead, for example, could be paraphrased in terms of the solidity of the core and the absence of volcanic activity. And there is something compelling in the position that if a metaphor has empirical content, if it expresses a substantive *proposition*, then that content, that proposition, must be expressible in *non*metaphorical terminology. What, after all, would a proposition be like which could *not* be literally expressed? But this requirement, which seems so clear at first, becomes obscure when pressed; for the precise force of 'literal' is not straightforward. If meeting the requirement of literal translatability means doing more than passing the objectivity tests mentioned above, then it is too stringent for a reasonable empiricism. We cannot reasonably require more of a metaphor than we do of literal expressions. If 'explosive temper' and 'green recruit' are as intersubjective and unproblematic in use as 'magenta,' 'cloudy,' and 'loud,' that should be enough to show parallel descriptive force. If it does not mean more than that, however, it then appears in a totally new light: for surely there need not be terminology extant to conveniently paraphrase precisely that insight found in a legitimate, objective, expository metaphor. Presumably a very important part of the reason languages evolve is that situations keep arising in which it becomes important to say things that we cannot say without some revision of the present language.[5] And an objective metaphorical statement could easily express one of these 'at the time' untranslatable things—without offense. Furthermore, it could be that the thing (phenomenon, aspect, etc.) picked out by the metaphor had not even been explicitly *noticed* before the advent of the metaphor, in which case we would have had no concept to *have* a literal expression of until that time. And it might well be the case that the concept in question is one of those that requires some ostensive familiarity in order even to get it into a language (the classic example is color, but there are an indefinitely large number of them: tones, aches, textures, odors, and much that is complex or subtle in the behavior of things). So if, prior to a certain metaphorical device, that ostensive familiarity as a matter of fact was simply not available, if there was simply no existing linguistic institution capable of drawing attention specifically to it, then the precise point of the metaphorical proposition might have been simply unformulable.

But where does that leave us? Can we still insist on a literal paraphrase? In a sense, I think we can; but it is a very interesting sense.

Good expository metaphors are mortal: among them we can distinguish the quick and the dead. 'Dead metaphor' was a pejorative for Orwell, but that was in another context and for another point. In analytic philosophy it might well be considered a term of praise: at the very least 'mortal' is laudatory. A metaphor dies when the metaphorically extended use of a term becomes established more or less independently of the original paradigm. Perhaps because of an unusual demand for the

5. Obviously, the revision may in some sense be describable (perhaps metaphorically!) "within" the language; but neology is nevertheless recognizable.

insight or appreciation afforded by the extended use, it will develop a life of its own. A new concept will be formed with its own characteristics, which are related to, but no longer logically so dependent upon the original use of the term. The original 'objectivity tests' will simply become application criteria. This is doubtless what happened in the case of 'guinea pig,' 'pollyanna,' 'toe the line,' 'jackknifed semitrailer,' and 'dry vermouth.' Sometimes the original use is completely dissociated and forgotten (which was Orwell's stylistic objection). But in death a metaphor becomes its own literal paraphrase: it takes on objective criteria of application just like any other literal expression. It may still be easiest to *teach* the use of the term by appeal to the old metaphor; but the application criteria will be the touchstone of understanding. And since this *could* happen to *any* objective metaphor, the requirement of literal translatability is automatically satisfied. So the mortality of a metaphor is the index of its substantive content: if it can pass the objectivity tests, the results of those tests can become application criteria for the term. And a dead metaphor has at least demonstrated its mortality.

The evolution of the very basic, explanatory concepts of scientific theory, which was briefly described in the Introduction, can be characterized in terms of the death of metaphors and the consequent specification of their explanatory insight. Many of the key terms in science mentioned there began their scientific life as groping metaphors, filled with suggestiveness, and died as a result of their explanatory success. The systematic scrutiny to which they are naturally subjected guarantees that scientific metaphors will be a model of empirical respectability. But the most interesting feature of the scientific examples is one almost wholly absent from the more pedestrian cases: as the scientific metaphor dies, as the new concept evolves, it gains in detail and precision. It takes on more and more definite shape. This peculiarity is a direct and understandable consequence of the explanatorily investigative nature of the scientific enterprise; and as pointed out earlier, it is more naturally referred to as 'discovering the properties of theoretical entities.' It is this feature, as much as anything else, which distinguishes science from the proto-scientific or merely rational activities of men.

The major point of this argument may now be set out: It will be the central contention of this essay that teleological expressions in most nonhuman applications represent dead anthropomorphic metaphors. The cases in which it is easiest to show the objective (intersubjective) applicability of these expressions are cases of elaborate goal-directedness in animals and mechanisms. But there are other sorts of cases that qualify, and those will be developed in later chapters. In general, I will argue that the feature of human teleology which transfers to nonhuman cases is the fact that when we say 'A in order that B,' the relationship between A and B plays a role in bringing about A. It is this which is being pointed out, rather than intelligence and conscious purpose. In fact, just as in many of the nonteleological cases we have examined, it is usually so bizarre to suppose conscious intent in the nonhuman cases that nobody is seriously misled; the case is rather like dead planets and stale traffic lights. At the same time, since there is clearly no reversal of cause and effect in human cases, this argument in terms of metaphorical extension should have no tendency whatever to license such reversal in nonhuman cases.

The next natural question is, of course, 'What exactly *is* the relationship between A and B, and *what* role does it play in bringing about A?' Answering that question will be the task of the next two chapters. It will take two chapters because, I will contend, anthropomorphic metaphors have died in at least two distinct ways. Although it is very common to run them together, two different contexts have provided dying anthropomorphic metaphors with different precise detail. All this, of course, remains to be shown.

OBSTRUCTIONISM

Before leaving this discussion, a few words should be said about the third general objection to teleological explanations raised earlier: that scientific research would stop if scientists accepted such explanations. If the general theme of the immediately preceding argument is sustained throughout the rest of this essay, then I will have shown teleological conceptualizations to have an enormous amount in common with many important explanatory concepts in natural science. They will be shown to have no specifically logical or philosophical difficulties whatever. Accordingly, if their acceptance would in fact bring about the end of scientific research, we might well place the blame on the scientists, not the concepts. If, however, the end of research is forecast on the basis of a misunderstanding of teleological concepts and their role in empirical inquiry, then the argument prosecuted here may well provide just the weapon needed to defeat that dire prediction.

CHAPTER II

THE DIRECTION OF BEHAVIOR

In light of the argument in the last chapter, the most important observation to be made about behavior directed toward a goal is that its goal-directedness is often obvious on its face. Many of our teleological judgments are as reliable and intersubjective as the run of normal perceptual judgments. Occasionally there simply is no question about it: the rabbit is fleeing, the cat stalking, the squirrel building a nest. Certain complex behavior patterns seem to demand teleological characterization. It is because of this that we have any reason at all to think that there is something to give a philosophical analysis of. The notion is interesting precisely because it functions so clearly in these contexts.

In this case, as in any other, the evidence we have for our perceptual competence may be colossally difficult to state in any detail; nevertheless it may be fairly obvious that the evidence is good. It is often clear, for example, that if our judgment were very far wrong, we would be confronted immediately by embarrassing consequences. We say the dog is chasing the rabbit, but he overtakes the rabbit and runs right by it; he then destroys himself by crashing full tilt into the first obstacle in his path. This is precisely the same sort of evidence we have for the reliability of our nonteleological perceptual identifications. They too are usually innocent of any formal testing; but it is clear how immediately we would be embarrassed if we were not *very* good at reliably identifying curbs, doors, and trucks-moving-rapidly-in-our-direction. The epistemological credentials of our perceptual skill in recognizing directed behavior are every bit as good as they are in these cases. We can simply *tell* that behavior is directed, that it has a goal, sometimes even what the goal is. If this is to invoke an anthropomorphic metaphor, it is unquestionably mortal.

Still, to show that we are objectively identifying something in these cases is not to say very much about what that something is. The teleological characterization of that something remains tendentious even after we have shown its *identification* to be reliably intersubjective. For it is the central logical property of teleological characterizations that they explain what they characterize. When we say 'A in order that B,' or 'A for the sake of B,' we ipso facto answer a question of the form 'Why A?' This is as true of functions as it is for goal-directed behavior, but here I am concerned only with the latter.[1] When I say the rabbit is running in order to escape from the dog, I am saying *why* the rabbit is behaving as it is. And since merely characterizing the behavior as fleeing implies that it takes place 'in order to escape. . . ,' this characterization itself offers an explanation. If the rabbit is not running in order to escape, it is not fleeing. Similarly for stalking, evading, and anything of the form 'trying to X.' So teleologically characterizing what we reliably identify in these instances places some constraints on it: it has to be explanatory of the behavior.[2] Accordingly, whatever else a general account of teleological behavior

---

1. The case for functions will be argued in the following chapter.

2. To put to rest fears that this is not the sort of thing that could possibly be reliably perceived, consider the fact that many ordinary causal diagnoses are nakedly perceptual in precisely this way. We can simply *tell* that firing the shotgun caused the hole in the door; we are incredibly reliable at saying, e.g., it was falling down the stairs that caused the pain. In each of these cases what we perceive is explanatory; we see not only what happened, but also why it happened.

must contain, it must at least provide the form of an explanation of this behavior; it must say something in general about why behavior of this sort takes place.

Among philosophers who have recognized this, there has been sharp disagreement concerning just what sort of explanation is being offered by teleological ascriptions. Some contend that the forward-oriented focus-on-a-goal characteristic of teleological explanations irreconcilably differentiates it from the essential perspective of "ordinary" causal explanation. This position has been defended both by those who take teleological explanations to be legitimate and respectable, and by those who do not. The latter usually argue that teleological explanations are illegitimate, not empirically respectable, precisely *because* they are not in any sense causal. The former, of course, hold that causal explanations are not the only legitimate kind of explanation in this context, and would offer in support the fact that teleological explanations, for instance, are both (obviously) legitimate and not causal.

On the other side of this issue are those who would contend that teleological explanation is nothing sui generis but merely a very special type of causal account. The position here would be that teleological explanations are causal in the very broad sense that they explain what produces or brings about the behavior in question; they offer an etiology.[3] The major problem from this perspective, of course, is specifying the kind of etiology which has the requisite teleological properties; and it is this that has led to the incredible Rube Goldberg complexity found in much of the empiricist literature on teleology.

3. Although 'etiology' has impeccable credentials, both lexical and etymological, for the use I have given it here, it is worth mentioning that this use was suggested to me by the role the word 'etiology' plays in the field of medicine.

Relevantly, the sui generists' arguments are primarily negative. They hold that no etiology *can* have the right properties. For, first of all, teleological accounts of behavior and causal accounts of behavior are *rivals*: teleological explanations *contrast with* causal ones; one sort will *rule out* the other. Did you jump, or were you pushed? Did you do it, or did it happen to you? It simply could not be both; nothing could be clearer. Furthermore, this argument continues, the forward orientation of teleology—the feature primarily responsible for this contrast—is hostile to the whole causal perspective. Attempting to assimilate cause and teleology must therefore rest on a fundamental misunderstanding.

But all this argument really shows is that certain specific etiologies are clearly inconsistent with certain teleological characterizations. And displaying cases of incompatibility does not show the sui generists' desiderata cannot be met within an etiological analysis. At this point, however, the arguments for assimilating causal and teleological characterizations usually become analogical and programmatic. If we accept *human* teleology as paradigmatic, for example, and expect the *form* of the explanation to transfer (as opposed to the specifically human attributed), then other teleological explanations should share the salient logical features of action explanations. And explanations of human behavior in terms of reasons, motives, purpose, and intent are plainly etiological: they help us understand what brought about the behavior in question.[4]

Of course, there are two important advantages that would accrue to an etiological analysis. First, if it can be

---

4. Compelling arguments to this effect have been made by two antimechanists, who one would expect to be most sensitive to the sui generists' position. These are, C. Taylor *in* "Explaining Action," *Inquiry* 13:54-89, and N. Malcolm *in* "The Conceivability of Mechanism," *The Philosophical Review* 77:45-72.

shown that teleological explanation is merely a species of (broadly) causal explanation, disputes over whether teleological explanations are legitimate or really explanatory will have thereby ended. They would have been shown to be explanations in a quite generally acceptable sense of that term, in no need of semantic apology or defense against pun. Second, and relatedly, this assimilation would allow us to avoid rather easily the logical and methodological difficulties that have sometimes beset the sui generists: namely, eschatology, and the temptation to post-hoc-ergo-propter-hoc arguments. The charges lodged by Kins Collins against Marx in chapter one, for example, could never be made in the name of teleology if it were provided with an etiological analysis. Experimental techniques and argumentative caveats that are already well developed could simply be reapplied to guide teleological characterizations, and hence to identify and avoid these potential logical derangements.

Considerations such as these originally encouraged me to embark on the project of this essay. These same considerations provide reason to take cheer at its central contention: that the sui generist position is groundless. This chapter and the next will be devoted to identifying the kind of etiologies that have teleological properties; they will give substance to the claim that the causal/teleological distinction is a distinction among etiologies, rather than between etiologies and something else; and they will do this in a way that accommodates a robust, forward-oriented focus on consequences as a primary characteristic of teleological explanations.

The very general observation that teleological ascriptions are ipso facto explanatory, together with the identificatory considerations with which this chapter opened, form the kernel around which I propose to build an analysis. It is interesting that understanding the analytical interplay between the explanatory and the identificatory aspects of teleological conceptualizations helps bring some order to the dazzling welter of teleological analyses produced by philosophers in the last half-century: some have underrated (or altogether ignored) one feature, some the other; and each misstep has been the source of much confusion and difficulty. I shall not, however, here attempt anything like a general survey of the literature from this perspective. I will examine the literature on these points only when it will help lubricate the argumentative machinery.

THREE CLASSIC ANALYSES

The three classic 'empiricist' analyses of teleological behavior offered in the last few decades all yield teleological characterizations that are explanatory of the behavior they characterize. And for the authors of *these* analyses, it almost goes without saying that the explanations are etiological. N. Wiener et al.[5] gave us the famous cybernetic analysis in terms of feedback devices. And machinery digesting signals that rush to and from a goal-object represent the very paradigm of an underlying causal account of behavior. So if just saying behavior is goal-directed commits us to an underlying feedback mechanism, then so characterizing the behavior provides an etiology. The equally renowned analyses of R. B. Braithwaite[6] and Ernest Nagel,[7] while not tying their

5. "Behavior, Purpose and Teleology," *Philosophy of Science* X:18-24.
6. *Scientific Explanation* (Cambridge: Cambridge University Press, 1953).
7. *The Structure of Science* (New York: Harcourt, Brace and World, 1961).

analyses to a specific sort of device, are describable in very similar terms. Both take as fundamental the existence of causal laws linking serial state-descriptions of the system under consideration. The feature that labels a certain system 'teleological' for Braithwaite is the variety of starting points from which it will reach the same (type of) final state. By contrast, Nagel takes the distinguishing feature of teleological systems to be the ability to maintain a state in the face of certain causally relevant changes.[8] This difference, as John Canfield has pointed out,[9] is merely a difference in paradigms, not in detailed ramification. Braithwaite takes pursuit as his model, Nagel homeostasis; but each claims to be able to handle all the cases of the other sort by suitable choice of parameters. In any case, it is clear that both analyses are etiological: the very identification of teleological behavior is at bottom a matter of determining the underlying causal regularities and boundary conditions which conspire to produce it. It is boringly orthodox to point out that such characterizations are essentially explanatory: the explanation in each case is of the standard covering-law/causal-deterministic kind.

Unfortunately, these analyses cannot accommodate a substantial range of clear and objective goal-directed behavior, and furthermore, they manage to include a range of demonstrably nonteleological behavior as well. A fortiori, they cannot allay the sui generists' fears that the requisite distinction can never be made within an etiological analysis. Some of the clearest cases of goal-directedness consist in unsuccessful attempts and searches launched for a nonexistent goal. Among other difficul-

8. For a fuller discussion of these analyses see "The Case Against Teleological Reductionism," *British Journal for the Philosophy of Science* 19:211-223.

9. *Purpose in Nature* (Englewood Cliffs, N.J., Prentice-Hall, 1966), Introduction.

ties, none of the above analyses can handle both these kinds of case.[10] But it is crucial to notice that, quite independent of any other considerations, it is precisely their preoccupation with the underlying structural detail which discomfits these analyses as adequate general characterizations of goal-directedness. This is so for two reasons. First, describing behavior teleologically—saying it is directed toward a certain goal—usually does not commit us to an exact function relating position or state description to time. Usually, from the point of view of an underlying causal-deterministic account, a teleological characterization only restricts behavior to a certain range, providing us with certain broad constraints. Accordingly, within the appropriate range, determinism can fail without affecting the goal-directedness of the behavior. This alone prevents any deterministic substructure-unpacking from producing the desired result. But there is another consideration in virtue of which we should have expected analyses of the above sort to have been wide of the mark.

Each of these classic analyses has neglected what I have called the identificatory consideration: the teleological attributions resulting from casual inspection often possess a remarkable degree of reliability and intersubjectivity. One of the chief things an analysis of teleological behavior must account for is the fact that we are reliably able to make the distinction in so many cases; the fleeing, stalking, searching, building, homing and mating, of men and pets, insects and mechanisms, are the very paradigms of teleological behavior. Accordingly, we should

10. The classic catalog of these accommodation difficulties can be found in Israel Scheffler's "Thoughts on Teleology," *British Journal for the Philosophy of Science* 9. I have discussed these and other difficulties in "The Case Against Teleological Reductionism," *ibid.*

view with suspicion any analysis that contends that goal-directedness consists in a relationship among parameters of which we are usually quite ignorant in the contexts of these reliable judgments. And in these cases we simply do not know the laws and state descriptions, the causal chain and variency, the underlying mechanism. Without further argument then, an analysis in terms of coarser, more rudimentarily perceptual aspects of behavior would be vastly more plausible.

THE TAYLOR ANALYSIS

From this vantage, the analysis of teleological behavior offered by Charles Taylor in *The Explanation of Behaviour*[11] represents a big step in just the right direction. His analysis, while still etiological, offers us something much further removed from the details of an underlying mechanism than any that went before it. For Taylor, behavior is goal-directed, occurs for the sake of some end, simply if it occurs because it is required for this end. To account for behavior teleologically is to ". . . account for it by laws in terms of which an event's occurring is held to be dependent on that event's being required for some end." The etiological nature of this analysis becomes clearer as Taylor's elaboration becomes more detailed.

. . .(teleological) behaviour is a function of the state of the system and its environment; but the relevant feature of the system and environment on which behaviour depends will be what the condition of both makes necessary if the end concerned is to be realized. [*The Explanation of Behaviour,* p. 9]

11. (London: Routledge and Kegan Paul, 1964.)

On this view, teleological behavior has what might be called a 'requirement etiology': what brings it about is its being required. As Taylor insists, it is often perfectly observable that a specific sort of behavior is what is required for a certain end. In fact, Taylor's formulation sounds like something we would naturally say in embellishing and supporting our teleological characterizations in actual cases. "Why did he do that?" "He *had* to do that if he was to avoid getting caught." So if we can use this kind of formulation as the basis of a philosophical analysis, we will have strong assurance at the outset that the analysis will offer us some insight into these macroscopic identificatory features of teleological behavior which are the source of our interest.

Although there are some problems in Taylor's view as formulated above, these rather idiomatic formulations are actually less problematic than, and generally preferable to the 'strict' version Taylor eventually defends in *The Explanation of Behaviour*. There he evidently feels uneasy about using an unanalyzed notion of causal dependency (occurs *because*...), and, in the formulation he settles on, he substitutes for this notion an analysis of it in terms of a qualified sufficient condition. This is an unfortunate move, for it admits a whole array of objections and counterexamples which the more idiomatic formulations avoid, inter alia a relative of the 'multiple goals' difficulty that Scheffler marshals against Braithwaite.[12] And it is just one more instance of an unhappy tendency in the literature of analytical philosophy to feel that the unanalyzed notion of a causal connection is logically so septic that it should always be avoided in favor of some — almost *any* — reduction formula.

12. I raise a number of these difficulties in "Explanation and Teleology," *Philosophy of Science* 39:204-218.

This tendency is unhappy for two reasons. First, no-
where in the literature is there an analysis of cause —
simple or complex — that captures enough of the concept
to be a workable substitute for the notion itself in any
context in which it plays a significant role. Furthermore,
this situation is almost certain to continue indefinitely;
for the more sophisticated the analyses become, the
clearer becomes the conclusion that the notion of a causal
connection is such a primitive conception that we may
never be able to say anything about it which is at the same
time both true and informative. And as the analyses get
better it also becomes clearer that the eventual result of
the process will never be anything anyone would want to
substitute for the unanalyzed conception in any analytical
application: it will likely be some colossally rococo night-
mare that will take several pages to write down, and
much tutoring to understand.[13] Second, the worry that
drives philosophers to such extreme analytical lengths,
and sponsors the employment of palpably inadequate for-
mulas, is, as far as I can see, wholly unjustified. For the
techniques necessary to display objectively the existence
of a causal connection are so highly developed and re-
fined that it of all things should be able to function in our
analyses without further comment. Analysis has to stop
somewhere, of course; and when we get to something as
objectively demonstrable as is a causal connection in a
vast array of useful cases, we should at least have the per-
spicacity to stop there: we are not likely to find anything
better. Certainly this counsel is preferable to going down

13. A mere glance at the literature of the past decade will serve to underscore this
point. But see especially, Marc-wogau, K., "On Historical Explanation," *Theoria* 28:
213-233; J.L. Mackie, "Causes and Conditions," *American Philosophical Quarterly* 2:
245-264; M. Scriven, "On the Concept of Cause," *Theory and Decision* 2:49-66; and
D. Davidson, "Causal Relations," *Journal of Philosophy* 64:691-703.

with an attractive oversimplification under a hail of counterexamples.

In Taylor's case it is instructive to note that the features of the sufficient condition account of cause which raise difficulties for him are the standard ones. First, since there are noncausal guarantees, and cases of overdetermination, something must be included to distinguish sufficient conditions that are causal (explanatory) from those that are not. Second, in order for the sufficiency to remain physical (contingent) and not devolve to tautology, some way must be found to rule out an indefinitely large number of interfering factors. Hand waving in either case, such as Taylor's allowing exceptions to the sufficiency if they are 'cogent,' merely returns us to zero: it essentially relies on our ability to recognize *really* causal cases when we see them.

Accordingly, I propose to build an analysis of teleological behavior upon Taylor's more informal formulation: behavior is teleological when it arises because it is required; teleological etiologies are requirement-etiologies. Even this formulation has some problems; but it is the first one to meet both the explanatory and the identificatory desiderata, and it does avoid a number of internal difficulties which Taylor's 'stricter' formulation does not. In point of fact Taylor's insight here is far more exciting than it at first appears. For the analysis that develops out of this insight will account for virtually all the important preanalytic features of teleological characterizations and teleological explanations of behavior. It provides for the classic forward orientation of teleological characterizations, the contrast between teleological and 'merely' causal explanations, and the consistency of teleological explanations with an underlying mechanistic indeterminacy. It shows how the consequences of a teleological bit

of behavior can function in its own etiology, how teleological behavior can be the legitimate object of direct
observation, and why such behavior can be directly and
reliably observed only in certain special contexts. And in
a way closely related to this last point, it provides a very
plausible account of trying behavior and of anthropomorphic insight. Moreover, it does this in a way that
makes goal-directedness a perfectly respectable empirical
notion.

MODIFYING THE TAYLOR FORMULA

As it stands, the 'because it is required' formula is at best
a sufficient condition for behavior to be teleological; it is
very far from necessary. Nothing a predator does by way
of stalking is in any strong sense *required* for the goal of
food, although the activity is clearly purposive. Prey may
be trapped or found dead; or it might accidentally walk
into a predator's unsuspecting clutches; or some fairly
unsophisticated trickery might result in the same end
without stalking. It is interesting that Taylor recognizes
this. He is prepared to admit that in many cases there
may be a number of different activities that would result
in the achievement of a given end, and that these are normally selected among by appeal to some principle such as
least effort. But he thinks his formulation can be saved
simply by including the selection criterion in the behavioral context so that we may "generally assume the selection has been made, and speak elliptically of 'the event
required for' the goal or end." (*The Explanation of Behavior*, p. 9n) As ingenious as this is, it still will not do.
For as long as accidents are possible, an end may be satisfied without employing *anything* in the organism's repertoire of purposive activities. *None* is required, even if we

include the selection criterion in the context. Furthermore, the selection could be essentially random, in which
case there would be no criterion and the same result
would ensue.

It might still be argued that 'what's required' is a per-
ceptually applicable predicate only very tenuously related
to the notion of necessity. And, as will become clear below, I would not object to that sort of move at all, as a
matter of principle. I will, however, argue that there are
far better ways of expressing this, and, further, that it is
preferable to think of there being several related predicates, rather than just one.

Moreover, Taylor's particular invocation of the notion
of requirement cannot be given this construction. For he
is driven to this formulation by a curious and unfortunately widespread prejudice about the nature of explanation, namely, that the explanation of P, the answer to the
question 'Why did P occur?,' must itself rule out all alternatives to P; that is to say, the explanation itself must be
inconsistent with not-P. This in turn has led to the 'deductive requirement': that part of an explanation be an argument to the effect *that* P (must) occur. But this is a caricature of our usual explanations. Explanations of P, answers
to the question 'Why did P occur?' invariably *presuppose*
that P did occur, and contain nothing that would count as
an argument *that* P occurred, except very trivial and uninteresting ones. Usually they lean so heavily on the fact
that P occurred as to completely disqualify themselves
from supporting the claim that it did. In any case, to say
that the train wreck occurred because of the bent rail, to
explain the house fire as the result of spontaneous combustion, to say that Johnny caught measles because he
was exposed to Jimmy, is not directly to appeal to anything logically inconsistent with any of those things not

happening. And *this* is the sort of explanatory force I take teleological ascriptions to have. This is the force of 'because' in 'it occurred because it was required.' If we can show teleological ascriptions to provide this kind of explanation we will have shown a great deal. We will then have assimilated them to something it is far more difficult to impugn. So I take it that there is no reason to accede to Taylor's hardnosedness here, and every reason to resist.

As might be expected, it turns out that successful teleological behavior, directed behavior that actually achieves its goal, provides us with the best paradigm; it gives us the sort of case from which all others can be seen as natural derivatives. Consider the rabbit escaping from a dog by darting through a hole in the fence. By viewing this behavior teleologically, we are implicitly saying something about its etiology; we are saying something about why it was that just that particular bit of behavior was exhibited just then by that animal. And since we could still maintain that the behavior was goal-directed even if there were several holes in several fences, we cannot be saying that the behavior arose because it was required for escape. Rather, all we are saying is that the behavior in question arose because it would *in fact* effect escape. We might be able to explain why the rabbit chose this particular course as opposed to open alternatives that would have worked as well, but we might not. That does not matter. All the (paradigmatic) teleological characterization commits us to is that the behavior in question *had* the requisite property (would effect escape), and that it arose *because* it had that property. The rabbit ran through the hole in the fence *because* doing that would allow it to escape from the dog.

In cases in which there are alternative courses open, it is perhaps more natural to phrase this, "the behavior occurs because it is the *sort of thing* that will bring about the goal." This formulation is nearly identical to one Taylor used before settling on the 'requirement' formulation. But more important, it leads naturally to the first of a series of modifications necessary to link the paradigm to the cases I am calling 'derivative.'

Clearly, much teleological behavior does *not* guarantee the achievement of its goal, and some of it is plainly unsuccessful. The fence might be too far away to reach safely, or the hole might be too small, or even covered by plate glass. Nevertheless, the behavior in such cases could still be 'for the sake of' or 'in order to' escape. So the operative property must be relaxed to accommodate these cases. We might say that the behavior occurred because it is the sort of thing that *tends* to bring about a certain goal. Or, getting increasingly anthropomorphic, it occurs because it is the right sort of thing to try in these circumstances. The sense of these modifications is sometimes captured by saying that the behavior was *appropriate*, given the goal, though unsuccessful, inept or even impossible from the outset. In these cases we would say the behavior occurred *because* it was appropriate, for that goal.

Since on this analysis the etiologically operative property of teleological behavior (would lead to X, be appropriate for X, and so forth) generally concerns the consequences of that behavior, I have chosen to call teleological etiologies 'consequence-etiologies.' A moment's reflection will reveal that Taylor's requirement-etiologies are a species of consequence-etiology: the behavior is required if the right consequences are to ensue. So in general we may say that teleological behavior is behavior with a consequence-etiology; and behavior with a consequence etiology is behavior that occurs because it brings about, is the type of thing that brings about, tends to bring about, is required to bring about, or is in some other way appropriate for bringing about some specific goal. Allowing the 'tends to' terminology to represent this entire 'family,' we can easily formulate the modified Taylor formula thus:

> S does B for the sake of G iff:
>   (i) B tends to bring about G.
>   (ii) B occurs because (i.e., is brought about by   (T)
>   the fact that) it tends to bring about G.

(Let me refer to this formula as '(T).') This way of putting it may look frighteningly difficult to apply in concrete cases, and that may be what led Taylor to his more precise, albeit less defensible formulation. The question of objective application will occupy us shortly. For now it is important only to recognize that this fuzzy-looking statement is the best that can be done. If Taylor's analysis is interpreted liberally enough to cover the tough cases, it simply ends up looking like (T). If not, it must be replaced by this analysis.

TESTABILITY

One of Taylor's two main claims for his analysis is that it avoids the charge of empirical undecidability which functioned so centrally in the vitalist controversy earlier this century. He claims, as I mentioned, that whether or not something is required for something else is often the legitimate object of direct observation. Consequently, whether or not this requirement, barring interference, is responsible for the occurrence of some specific behavior should be testable, empirically determinable. If so, the crucial question now becomes: does this property of the

analysis survive my modification? Is my looser formulation empirically demonstrable?

Since even *speaking* of behavior teleologically (stalking,
fleeing) presupposes the applicability of (T), we must
begin such a demonstration with behavior described nonteleologically. Let me use the term 'physico-geometrical'
to represent this sort of description. Now the behavior we
are concerned with here—that to be characterized and
explained teleologically—can, from a physico-geometrical point of view, be of a wide variety of different kinds. It
can be a certain path or set of paths (pattern); it can be
stationary gesticulation, or it can be some other configurational change or pattern of changes; and of course it
can be the complete absence of motion and change; and
it can be motion or motionlessness with respect to virtually anything in the environment. Such behavior is
quite often referred by the use of a demonstrative pronoun in its presence. And the adequacy of any descriptive
expression nearly always requires and presumes an ostensive familiarity with the behavior. "Why did he do that?"
"What?" "What he just did, you know, go up to the edge,
stop, and flail the water all frothy." "Oh, that. He was
just trying to attract attention."

Whether a bit of physico-geometrically characterized
behavior will have the property we are interested in—
whether it tends to bring about G—will usually depend
on some details of the environment. Whether a certain
path will lead to prey or effect escape obviously depends,
inter alia, on the nature and location of obstacles, and
other agents. So, by altering these features of the environment we can change precisely that property of the behavior on which the application of (T) depends. Hence if we
can show that the occurrence of a particular bit of behavior *depends on* the environment being such that the

behavior has that property, we have empirically demonstrated that the formula applies: the behavior is directed towards G.

Given the force of 'because' and 'brings about' (and 'etiology') in this analysis, the demonstration that a bit of behavior, B, occurred because it would tend to bring about some goal G is methodologically indistinguishable from the demonstration of standard, orthodox causal links. A series of parallels will help make this clear.

A. At first, let us just consider the most straightforward sort of case that would satisfy (T): B occurs because it brings about (will bring about) G. Even here there are several distinct points to be made:

1. Suppose we can arrange an experimental environment such that at any one time there is only one (physico-geometrically specified) B which would achieve G, but that (by changing features of the setup) the B which would achieve G may be changed from time to time. For example, the escape route from a certain area could be altered in contour or direction by moving objects around. Suppose in addition that whenever the experiment is run (e.g., predator introduced) the B that achieves G occurs (e.g., the escape route is successfully taken). Now to demonstrate to a skeptic that the particular B that occurs, occurs *because* it is the one that will bring about G is like showing, say, that it really was the removal of the coil wire which caused the car's motor to stop (which also will occur every time in certain circumstances).[14] In general what is required is the elimination of alternative accounts of the phenomenon. If we suspect that there is

14. Even some peripheral details are interestingly similar in these cases: Just as someone familiar with automobiles might be incredulous at the possibility of a skeptic about coil wires, so too anyone the least familiar with animals would find doubts that a dramatic instance of flight behavior occurred *because* it would (tend to) produce escape hard to accept as genuine.

something about the way in which the coil wire is removed, which is independently killing the motor, we may try removing the wire in different ways or using different devices, and we could move the ignition circuitry around to change as many incidental relationships as possible. We might even try securing the wire badly and driving until it falls out by itself. This would minimize the likelihood of an enormous class of rival accounts, including ruse: for example, someone conspiring with the experimenter. Similarly, if we suspect that there is something in the order in which the different escape routes succeed each other that influences the occurrence of the particular Bs, we may randomly change that order and repeat the sequence a number of times. To systematically eliminate other ranges of alternative accounts we could change the colors, substances, shapes, and sizes of the environmental objects (e.g., those that define the escape route). And to eliminate the influence of more complex concomitants we could dream up radically novel things that would count as achieving G (e.g., an unusual form of safety). In this manner we could assure ourselves that a particular B occurs because it leads to escape, for example, just as certainly as yanking out the coil wire brings the motor to a halt. The sentence "If you make that hole too small for the predator to get in, X (the subject of our experiment) will be over here so fast it'll make your head swim," can have the same epistemological credentials as "Don't pull on that wire, you'll stop the motor."

2. A more realistic kind of case may be treated by expansion. In environments in which there is some B that would achieve G, there usually are several: for instance a class of distinct escape routes. Here there is the possibility that overlap of these classes will vitiate the consequence-

etiological interpretation of an otherwise successful experiment. But this is obviated with a little care: for example, the use of nonoverlapping classes, or, if that is undesirable, at least being on guard for the systematic occurrence of B in the overlapping regions. This of course is simply a specific application of the general experimental admonition to eliminate alternative explanations, and hence does not in principle differentiate this sort of case from those discussed above. What is of interest in this sort of case concerns the selection of a specific B from within a class.

(a) It is possible that once the class of Bs which will achieve G is determined by the environment, the particular B that actually occurs is wholly random: duplicating the experimental conditions yields results essentially indistinguishable from a quantum-randomizer's explicit choices among the members. In this case all that can be said is that B occurred because it was the sort of thing that would bring about G, because it was one of those that would do it: no further account can be given. And contrary to one popular view, this randomness does not discomfit the consequence-etiological account. It would be fatuous to deny that Charlie's slamming the window caused the pane to break *simply* because we cannot say why the other panes in that window did not break. Even if it were completely random which one broke, or how many broke on a hard slam, it is still the slam that causes the breakage, and Charlie should be admonished to take it easy. So there is nothing terribly heterodox here in saying B occurred because it was something that would bring about G.

(b) In contrast, it might be the case that the particular B that occurs is not random. It might be determined by some principle such as Taylor's least-effort principle.

The escape route, for example, might consistently be the shortest, the lowest, the farthest from danger. Now it is sometimes thought that if such a principle *were* governing the occurrence of (a particular) B, then merely saying "B because it would result in G" is incomplete, inadequate, or in some other way incorrect. But this is not so. Neither would we deny that slamming caused the pane to break simply because there *was* a discoverable factor explaining why number 7 broke and not the others. Every causal inquiry ignores some questions, some factors, under headings like, "interesting but not central," or "distracting and obfuscatory." And there are contexts in which "because it would achieve G" is adequate, even if there are other things one could go on to say. Just as there are contexts in which "Charlie slammed it" is adequate even if shockwave propagation and crystal structure fascinates some people. Consider this exchange about a commotion in a fish tank. "Why did he do that?" "Oh, he was just cleaning that stuff off his back." This reply is adequate even though there are obviously a number of different ways he could have removed the offending substance. The questioner's concern might have been rightly perceived to be whether the object of his query was in the throes of death (hence no consequence-etiology) or, perhaps, beginning a rare mating ritual (different consequence-etiology). In this case, beginning the reply by distinguishing among the various ways in which something might be removed from a back, and invoking a principle in virtue of which they might be distinguished among, would risk excruciating puzzlement, possibly even fatal coma.

B. A further relaxation of the conditions imposed under A is required to accommodate certain failures of perception and execution: there are many ways in which behavior can fail its evident goal and still be directed toward it. In this case we invoke the more controversial disjuncts in Tii, saying that the behavior exhibited was plausible, appropriate, the right sort of thing given G, even though the performance was flawed. Two questions arise concerning these propriety judgments which must be treated here: (1) can these judgments be made objectively? and (2) do they have the requisite dependence on consequences?

1. To be objective enough to function in an experimental test, all that is required of propriety judgments is that they be as repeatable and intersubjective as the run of more orthodox perceptual judgments; and this they clearly are. In the proper context, it will be obvious to any reasonably experienced observer that jumping over a fence, or, perhaps, dashing through a hole in a rock, is appropriate escape behavior, and this is true even if the attempt is unsuccessful (a net is waiting on the other side). The repeatability and intersubjectivity of this judgment will easily be as good as the judgment, say, that the anode has begun to glow, or that the precipitate has formed, in a physics or chemistry lab. The fact that one must have experience to make objective propriety judgments does not differentiate them from any perceptions whatever, and especially not from experimental observations in the hard sciences. But that this experience is sometimes characterized by suspicious anthropomorphisms does deserve comment.

Once again, the behavior judged appropriate in a test must be specifiable in physico-geometrical terms: a path, configurational change, or pattern. We might, however, be able to consistently *recognize* such behavior as appropriate only (or most easily) if we "put ourself in its place (the place of the behaving object)" and think of the behavior as "just what I would have done," or "certainly reasonable," or, more elaborately that "it couldn't have seen that it wouldn't work." But so long as we can pass the perceptual reliability tests, it does not matter in the least what sort of device we use to help us master the skill. Just as it does not matter in the least what bizarre things go through your head when you are taking square roots, so long as you always get the answer right you have an objective skill. Moreover, anthropomorphic devices are used extensively in training the perceptions of students of respectable disciplines, with great benefit, and without sacrificing our ability to tell when they have it right. Electrical engineers are asked to think about what a circuit *sees* when it is connected in a certain way to another circuit. Mechanical engineers are told that a suspension system has no way of *knowing* whether its deflection is the result of a bump or of roll. And fatigue is a very helpful metaphor for students of metallurgy. None of this impugns the value of the lessons learned.

2. To show that the occurrence of B depends on its having an objective, if esoteric property, however, is not enough to show that it has a consequence-etiology. Using the word 'propriety' to refer to this property implies that it is a function of the goal, G, but nothing in the objectivity test requires that this be so. Nevertheless, the link between propriety and goal is established in the same manner as the objectivity of the propriety judgment itself. We must have (or find) evidence that the judgment depends on the goal, and the most straightforward way to do this is to have the same bit of behavior exhibited in different contexts, contexts that provide or suggest different goals. If we find that propriety judgments vary with goals in a repeatable and intersubjective way, we will have done all that is necessary.

Once again, it is safe to say that we all can pass some of these tests: if we are told that the beast darting through a hole is not fleeing a predator but rather looking for food, immediately our propriety judgment is less certain. And if we then notice that food has been placed near its original position, our judgment becomes negative — at least until further compelling detail is provided. Accordingly, without invoking anything but orthodox experimental principles, we can objectively establish that something is doing what it is doing *because* that is appropriate for a certain goal, even though it never attains that goal. Another way of putting this is to say that we can objectively discover what something is *trying* to do. It is just this that the '...tends to...' terminology in (T) is intended to capture: if behavior is appropriate vis-a-vis the achievement of G then it moves things in the right direction; at least from some vantage point, it tends to get the job done.

It is sometimes thought that propriety considerations of the sort detailed here introduce an essential and irreducible subjective element into the analysis: the perspective of an agent. If we allow anthropomorphic constructions of the sort I have already underwritten, then *any* behavior can be appropriate in a fixed set of circumstances, given the requisite presuppositions: namely, what beliefs about the state of affairs we attribute to the 'agent.' And this, some have argued, rules out any 'external' analysis of the sort I am propounding.

But this is a non sequitur. The analysis itself is neither external nor internal; all that must be external are the criteria for *applying* teleological concepts in explanatory contexts. And since we can sometimes determine what the presuppositions are, we can get an empirical handle on the 'agent's' perspective. Hence this objection does not

engage the argument I am presenting: sometimes there is
no objective, external way to determine the presuppositions of propriety—no way to discover the agent's perspective; but in these cases we simply must concede that
there is no way to determine the proper account of the
behavior either. All I am arguing is that there are other
times—other cases—in which all this *is* objectively determinable; it is in these cases that teleological concepts get
their empirical foothold.

Actually, the case is rather like more orthodox causal
accounts of behavior. We rely upon very general considerations, which we bring with us into the explanatory
situation, to rank presuppositions in order of antecedent
plausibility, and to thus choose among alternative
accounts of the behavior in question. "That animal is
(notoriously) skittish, so it is virtually certain that it was
trying to escape and just got confused." This is quite
parallel to, "that stuff is (famously) brittle, so it is super-
likely that the jolt was what broke it." In each case it is
possible (perhaps only barely) that we are mistaken; it is
possible that we are deceived. But any alternative
account of the matter would have to actually produce an
aspect of the case that raises problems for the proffered
account. Merely saying, for example, "well, it is possible
that it was already broken and just held together by a fortuitous magnetic field that dropped in intensity coincidentally with the jolt," is not enough for this alternative
to be considered a *serious* possibility. The same can be
said for, "well, it is possible that the animal did not see
the man (in spite of looking directly at him) and was actually frantically looking about for food."

Appropriate-but-unsuccessful behavior may well be
the most central kind of teleological behavior, both conceptually and identificatorily; for it is the behavior of

trying. And not only is trying one of the most emphatically teleological concepts but trying behavior constitutes the majority of that systematically complex behavior we are most reliable in identifying as teleological. The clearest cases of hunting, fleeing, and building consist largely of attempts—success is quite usually elusive. Furthermore, it is precisely trying behavior that functioned so centrally in Braithwaite's and Nagel's discussions under the headings of 'plasticity' and 'persistence,' which were there taken as the paradigms of objectively identifiable teleological behavior traits. What makes us say a predator is stalking—rather than writhing or undergoing spasms—is the systematic organization of the movements about the goal-object, or about the obvious clues to the goal-object, or about something that might be mistaken for a clue. It is this systematicity that makes the *direction* of the behavior so obvious. And the particular systematicity that gives direction to a bit of behavior is that which obtains when that behavior arises because it tends to produce a certain result, for example, the apprehension of prey. This kind of systematicity simply *is* plasticity and persistence of the sort Braithwaite and Nagel were concerned with, but misunderstood. If we were to conduct a giant Mill's Methods experiment to demonstrate that what was causing a certain kind of behavior in some context was that behavior's tendency to produce a certain result, the description of one successful outcome could be simply put: the behavior was plastic and persistent with respect to that result. Of course the detail of such an experiment would in general be enormously difficult to specify from what I have called the physico-geometrical point of view. So perhaps it is fortunate that it is at this end of the spectrum that our perceptions are most reliable.

It is clear, however, that the exact manner in which we break up behavior into individual "bits" or attempts is somewhat arbitrary. One smooth flow of action can often be viewed as consisting of a large number of individual *things* that were accomplished, all for the sake of some end. "Well, first he did this, then that, then this and this and that, which finally allowed him to do this, which was his goal all along." Accordingly, sometimes our extended perceptions themselves will have something like experimental form. We diagnose, or perhaps just make a stab at the goal, on the basis of one part of the behavior, and then see if it can accommodate the rest. Sometimes our perceptions will consist in a *series* of propriety judgments; and this provides fine-structure for the notions of plasticity and persistence in this context. I take the ease with which it handles trying behavior to be another significant advantage of (T) over Taylor's formulation.

Many of the preceding experimental points are nicely illustrated in E. S. Russell's rich collection of examples in *The Directiveness of Organic Activities.*[15] The one reproduced below was chosen more or less at random.

Experiments by Kepner and Barker have shown that *Microstoma* eats *Hydra* for the sake of its nematocysts rather than for its food value. Specimens containing few or no nematocysts attack *Hydra* readily; those with many or a full quota of nematocysts refuse *Hydra* for some days, even when hungry. One 'fully loaded' *Microstoma* which had been starved until it would accept *Hydra* digested the flesh of the *Hydra*, but rejected the nematocysts through its mouth. Conversely, a recently fed *Microstoma* with few nematocysts *may* reject the flesh of a *Hydra* it has eaten and retain the nematocysts. It appears therefore that need for the full complement of nematocysts is the main controlling factor inducing *Microstoma* to attack *Hydra*.

15. (London: Cambridge University Press, 1945.)

To which we might add: it then attacks *Hydra*, as opposed to other things, because *that* will (tend to) provide nematocysts. We would never say the attack was 'for the sake of nematocysts' if it were not the right sort of thing to do, given the 'need'; for example, if Hydra had no nematocysts to give. But the behavior is so obviously appropriate that Russell felt no need to mention it. This is a good example of the necessity (and the possibility!) of experimental resolution of ambiguity in the direction of behavior. Prior to the work of Kepner and Barker, it could plausibly have been maintained that Microstoma always attack Hydra for food, the nematocyst ingestion being merely a fortuitous concomitant. After the experimental work, that position could no longer be maintained. The direction of behavior had been empirically established.

SOME CONSEQUENCES

We are now in a position to take a second look at the charge of anthropomorphism and to examine another difficulty that has plagued discussions of teleology: the apparent circularity of teleological explanations. First anthropomorphism. Throughout this analysis I have been sympathetic to suspicious-sounding constructions that smack of "Well, that's how I would behave if I were there," as an elaboration of various aspects of our non-human teleological characterizations. This might seem to go far beyond anything I justified in the argument of the last chapter, and hence might seem to raise once again the specter of pernicious anthropomorphism. But it does not; and seeing why it does not will allow us to prosecute the argument of the last chapter one step further.

First of all, in a number of cases we have examined, no anthropomorphism whatever is involved in justifying a teleological ascription. The justification involves an antiseptic, causal investigation, invoking none of the suspicious locutions. So any *general* claim that teleology is perniciously anthropomorphic is clearly off target. The charge fails even to get an *apparent* purchase until we are forced to employ the propriety judgments that functioned so centrally in the above discussion. But here the purchase is merely superficial; for as we saw, these judgments need only be objective and reliable to serve adequately in (T) — they need not be nonanthropomorphic. Teleological behavior is not *simply* appropriate behavior: it is appropriate behavior *with a certain etiology*. Establishing the etiology is what is central to the teleological characterization. For this, all the etiologically operative property must be is, (a) objectively determinable, and (b) dependent upon the goal; it does not matter at all that the descriptions under which humans find it easiest to make these assessments happen to be anthropomorphic. All that matters is that they be intersubjectively testable; and this they assuredly are. There is nothing essentially subjective or mysterious about anthropomorphism of this sort.

There is, however, one area in which the charge might seem to carry more weight. In those cases in which our teleological characterizations themselves are a matter of causal inspection of the phenomenon (much of higher organic behavior), what we claim to be perceiving is the etiology itself, not just the propriety of the behavior. We *see* that the squirrel is building a nest, that the horse is going for the barn, and not just that the behavior is appropriate for nest-building or barn-going. Here it might be maintained that we are simply transferring pattern recognition skills from human contexts to non-human. Would this not be illicit, pernicious anthropomorphism?

Not necessarily. For here, as in perceptions generally, the reliability of our judgment is *everything*: to impugn a perceptual "skill" *merely* because it has anthropomorphic aspects, is to commit the genetic fallacy. We may quite legitimately rely upon anthropomorphic analogy to help us *recognize* complex behavior patterns. To determine, for example, whether the motion of a cat's ear is *for the sake of* increased hearing acuity, on the one hand, or a fear or irritation *reaction*, on the other, it may well help to 'put ourselves in its place' and characterize the situation 'from its point of view' and in terms of intentions, desires, hopes, and fears. The mistake (on both sides!) is only to confuse a recognition mnemonic with a justification. The anthropomorphic analogy may *explain our insight* into a complex phenomenon. The *justification of our teleological characterization*, however, must be that directive organization is the best etiological analysis or account of the movements; what is evoking them must be their tendency to produce a certain result. The correlation between this and our saying so is the *test* of our perceptual skill. And the discussion of (T) in the previous section provides the practical framework within which such a test may be conducted. If there is a question of human perceptual arrogance here, this should help combat it.

Before going on to the second difficulty, a generally valuable consequence of the foregoing discussion should be drawn. There is a strong epistemological parallel here between the concept of 'goal-directedness' and the class of concepts called 'theoretical' in philosophical discussions of the observational confirmation of theories. Theoretical terms, in this context, are taken to refer to things that are in some strong sense unobservable. Hence the *justification* for postulating them has to be that their existence *best explains* some phenomenon or other. Similarly, the justification for saying a certain bit of behavior is goal-directed has to be that the best explanation of the behavior is that it is being brought about by its tendency to produce a certain result. Furthermore, in some cases the goal-directedness of behavior is very difficult to detect (e.g., lower animals and plants). In these cases 'goal directedness' would simply *be* a theory term, being applied only after checking the consequences of its postulation.

This strong parallel may have been what tempted the vitalists to postulate an unobserved entity to direct the behavior of organisms toward a goal. The difficulty with that position is nearly classic, and I need not rehash it here. The real illumination provided by this parallel is on the observation/theory dispute. For it is clear that from a justificatory point of view, goal-directedness *always* satisfies the epistemological criteria for being a theory term: Saying that something is goal-directed is *justified* if goal-directedness (i.e., our formula) *is the best account of* that something's behavior. But it is *also* clear that in some cases, the goal-directedness of behavior is obvious, palpable, instantly recognizable, and unmistakable to the normally sighted individual, which is just to say it is observable. This suggests that from at least one very important perspective, 'theory-term' and 'observation-term' do not mark an *epistemological* distinction.

The second difficulty mentioned above probably attempts to articulate an uneasy feeling that there *must* be something circular about anything so involuted as the discussion of teleological systems on the last few pages. On

one hand, I offer the plasticity and persistence of the behavior of a system toward a certain result as the empirical
evidence demonstrating that the system has that result as
a goal. On the other hand, I clearly want to be able to say
we can *explain* the behavior of the system by appeal to its
having a certain goal. But how can I explain the behavior
of a system by appeal to its having a certain goal when the
evidence for its having that goal is a property of the behavior? Doesn't that really beg all the questions? Isn't that
circular?

I think that when the nature of such explanation is
properly understood — that is, in terms of (T) — it is clear
that whatever circularity there is, it is not vicious. First of
all, whether something S has goal G_1 is clearly an empirical issue. One merely has to determine whether (T) is true
when G_1 and S's behavior are substituted in it. And this
we saw was an empirical determination. But more important, (T) is true in this case only if S's behavior occurs
because it tends to bring about G_1. This is part of what is
meant by saying S has goal G_1. So just saying S has goal
G_1 is to offer an explanation of S's behavior. This is why
teleological explanations are *ascription*-explanations.
What looks like circularity is merely the natural invo-
lutedness of ascription-explanations: the content of the
modified Taylor formula is implicit in the simple statement that S *has* goal G.

INTERIM SUMMARY

I have been trying to show that (T) represents the best
way to put the insight of Charles Taylor's very perceptive
discussion of goal-directedness. Part of this has consisted
in showing that (T) satisfies a variety of desiderata: it ac-

commodates the explanatoriness of teleological characterizations and explicates the notion of ascription-explanation; it helps us understand why trying is such a central
teleological concept; it squares teleological explanations
with underlying causal indeterminacy; it accounts for the
role of anthropomorphism; and it shows how teleological
properties can be the legitimate object of direct observation. But there are two other features that any analysis of
the sort I am proposing should have. It should be able to
make some sense of the forward orientation of teleological explanations, and it should explicate the contrast
between teleological explanations and what might be
called 'merely' causal explanations. It is easy to show that
(T) can do both of these things.

Perhaps the most general feature of (T) is that it offers
consequence-etiologies as fundamental to teleological
explanation. It is this which allows us to account for the
forward-orientation of teleological accounts of behavior.
When we say that teleological etiologies are consequence-
etiologies, we are saying that the consequences of goal-
directed behavior are involved in its own etiology: such
behavior occurs *because* it has certain consequences. It
occurs because it tends to achieve G. That, quite simply,
is what the forward-orientation consists in: it is a focus on
consequences. And, as we saw, this involves nothing very
heterodox empirically. For example, in the experimental
context, the causally relevant *manipulation* takes place
before B, although the feature of that manipulation
which determines whether B will occur—that is, what
governs the occurrence of B—concerns what will ensue.
So B occurs *because* of what will ensue, but the statement
of the cause is always appropriately put in the future
tense: that things were such that G will (tend to) ensue.
And *this* statement concerns the state of affairs prior to B.

It is not surprising that precisely this same feature reveals the distinction between teleological explanations and explanations we call 'merely' causal. A merely causal explanation of B would provide an etiology in terms of the *antecedents* of B, not its consequences. The causal/teleological contrast is *among* etiologies, not between etiologies and something else. The form of a teleological explanation of B is: B does or tends to do thus-and-so, therefore B. A merely causal explanation of B would have the form: other sorts of things do or tend to do thus-and-so, therefore B. We may thus make empiricistically defensible sense of the Aristotelian distinction between efficient and final causes.

MECHANISM

It is common to view the teleological explanation of directed behavior as broadly dispositional. In general, this may come to no more than a recognition that we must have some way to express the variability of teleological responses to the same circumstances. Some things, we like to say, are 'disposed' to behave one way, some another, under a given set of conditions. Moreover, in a given set of circumstances, the very same teleological system will sometimes behave in one way, sometimes another, depending on what goal it has, or whether it has any at all. It is natural in light of this to think of teleological behavior as resulting from variable, active dispositions: natural tendencies to behave in certain ways.

From this perspective, (T) may be viewed as a general characterization of teleological dispositions. What differentiates teleological dispositions from ordinary ones (solubility, brittleness, etc.) is nothing more than the *form* of the feature on which they make the behavior depend. The usual sort of nonteleological disposition found, for example, in natural science, makes the behavior explained dependent upon a reasonably straightforward antecedent condition: being placed in a liquid, hit with a hard object, and the like. By contrast, behavior resulting from a teleological disposition depends upon antecedents that are systematically less straightforward, antecedents that are related to (and specifiable in terms of) the *consequences* of the behavior being explained. But the *dependency* is exactly the same: it is the usual sort of causal link, demonstrated using the same methodological principles. (T) allows us to see the empirical content of this disposition-talk, and shows us that there need be no question-begging in deciding when a disposition has changed. To this extent, the dispositional picture and (T) are quite congenial.

But it is sometimes thought that the dispositional picture of teleological explanation is incompatible with even a modest mechanism. It has been argued that explaining behavior teleologically, explaining it by appeal to anything like (T) which can be given this dispositional interpretation, simply rules out 'underlying' explanations in nonteleological terms of why the thing in question *was* disposed to behave in the way it was. (For example, a neurophysiological account of purposive, animate behavior would be impossible on this view.) And although this is a major issue, which will occupy us at some length later on, it will be valuable to show now, while the analysis is still fresh, two very important (and tempting) mistakes in arguments of this sort. These are arguments that concern teleological behavior in general, and do not concern specifically human teleology. Arguments in terms of specifically human *action* notions, such as intent and desire, will be treated elaborately in chapter four. For now, the light that (T) can shed on the more general case, and hence on mechanical and animate teleology, will be our primary concern. It will nevertheless be tendentious and engaging.

If (T) (or even something roughly like it) represents the proper analysis of goal-directedness, it is clear that the demonstration of the goal-directedness of something's behavior does not involve us at all in a discussion of the internal structure of that something. There is nothing within (T) or its demonstration which would prevent its application to a system S because of its internal nature. S could be an organism, a mechanism, a lump of quartz or a forest fire; so long as what S *did* could be shown to depend on its having certain consequences, S's behavior is teleological. But this alone does not show that S *cannot* have an inner nature, or B an underlying structure, which will offer an explanation of B in terms of its antecedents, rather than its consequences; for example, one in mechanical or neurophysiological terms. In fact, contrary to the reductionist views that attempt to identify teleological behavior with the mechanism producing it, the logical independence of a teleologically characterized B from any underlying mechanism[16] is just what we should expect if that underlying mechanism is to *explain* S's behavior; specifically if it is to explain why it is teleological. It is a peculiar explanans that follows deductively from its explanandum.

It is relatively easy to state the general conditions an underlying mechanistic account of S must meet in order to guarantee that S's behavior satisfy (T). S's manifesting behavior B_0 in environment E would be explained mecha-

16. 'Mechanism' represents any underlying, structural account, including neurophysiological ones.

nistically by appeal to the intrinsic[17] state description $(SE)_0$. S and E being in $(SE)_0$ would cause (i.e., make S do) B_0. However, S would be (or be designed) such that the B_0 it manifests in $(SE)_0$ would always satisfy (Ti). This is to say that S always does what tends to bring about G. Feedback mechanisms, of course, are clear illustrations of this schema. They are mechanically geared to their surroundings in such a way that, at least in some environments (e.g., after the missile is released in the presence of an appropriate target), the behavior the purely intrinsic mechanism causes them to manifest will always be something that tends to bring about some particular goal (e.g., the missile and the target being in the same place). It seems to follow that teleological behavior, goal-directed behavior, not only legitimately *can*, but sometimes actually *does* have an underlying intrinsic-mechanistic explanation. Sometimes it is the product of an underlying mechanism.

But even at this point it could be objected that I have run roughshod over some important distinctions: that there is something wrong with calling the behavior teleological, something wrong with saying it satisfies (T), if it is actually being produced by such a mechanism. For, it might be urged, its tendency to bring about G is *not* what's bringing about B_0 in this case. What is *really* producing B_0 is $(SE)_0$, which has nothing to do with B_0's consequences; so B_0 is really being brought about nonteleologically. B_0's tending to bring about G is merely an empirical correlate of its cause, and hence cannot be called upon to explain B_0's occurrence. It is like trying to

17. This is Taylor's term, which he defines (*The Explanation of Behavior*, p. 12) "without making any reference to. . .goals, e.g., by simply enumerating the components or by mentioning certain key stimuli which are impinging on. . .receptors." From our perspective, this term most importantly restricts considerations to things other than the consequences of B_0.

explain the searing of my hand by appeal to the redness of the hot coal, as opposed to its heat.

It is important to raise this objection here because it displays a fundamental misunderstanding of both cause and explanation, which, it seems to me, lies behind much of the confusion this subject has generated. It is certainly true, as this objection presumes, that there is a very close relationship between cause and explanatoriness: to give a cause is to give an explanation. As a number of philosophers have elaborately shown, however, choosing the explanatory factor — the cause — from among a number of empirical correlates, be they general, contextual, or accidental, is a subtle, conceptually complicated, and enormously context-dependent business.[18] The rules, if they are ever articulated, will not be anything like as straightforward as this objection requires. In a vessel of gas we can sometimes explain the rise in pressure by appeal to a rise in temperature, and sometimes vice-versa. It all depends on the particular circumstances, details of the context. Did we light the burner under the tank, or, alternatively, admit more gas? And if the vessel explodes following such a rise, we will sometimes explain it by appeal to T (temperature), sometimes by P (pressure), and sometimes by a weak seam in the vessel, depending on the situation. What the question, "Why did it explode?" asks in different cases will vary. What makes the hot coal example persuasive is, as Douglas Gasking has pointed out[19] the contingent fact, that while we can make a coal red by making it hot, nothing we know of counts as making it hot *by* making it red. It is a

18. See, e.g., the sources cited in n. 11 above, as well as, Nagel, *The Structure of Science*, p. 583 ff.; and M. Scriven, "Causes, Connections and Conditions in History," *Philosophical Analysis and History*, ed. W. Dray (New York: Harper and Row, 1966), pp. 238-264, especially pp. 254 ff.

19. "Causation and Recipes," *Mind* (1955), pp. 479-487.

question of manipulability. If we could make coals hot by directly manipulating their color, this case would be rather like the gas vessel, and hence lose even its apparent force.

But in addition to this sort of thing, there are also important considerations: nearly every causal judgment involves the separation of factors into instigational, instrumental, and incidental,[20] as well, perhaps, as other role categories and gradations. For example, in a train wreck, the instigational factor might be a bent rail, whereas, the fact that train wheels follow rails, while causally relevant, is merely incidental here. Which is to say it does not explanatorily isolate this case from those in which wrecks (like this one) do *not* occur. In the above explosions, one might be tempted to say, for example, that pressure was the "immediate cause" in every case; after all, it is the push of the pressure which makes an explosion. But frequently this immediacy is an explanatory liability, relegating the "immediate cause" to the status of mere instrumentality. It is very often fatuous in such cases to invoke the pressure as the cause of the explosion ("Yes of course the pressure must have gone up. What I want to know is what *caused* the thing"); and this is so precisely because it is too immediate: it does not tell us anything we did not already know, that is, it does not explain anything.

It is even more relevant to notice that the successful elaboration of the kinetic theory of matter in no way discomfits more pedestrian accounts of the above sorts of phenomena, in terms of macrothermodynamic concepts and paraphernalia, *in the contexts where they were previously appropriate*. In some contexts, "Why the explo-

---

20. I owe this alliterative trichotomy to Michael Scriven.

sion?" is adequately answered by, "Some jackass left the burner on too high," and injecting esoteric microphysics would be an impertinent bore. True, in this same context, answering the *further* question concerning why leaving burners too high causes explosions could well appeal to kinetic theory. But this, of course, *is* a *further* question. The original question was adequately answered; and there was nothing about the reply—the explanation —that required this further question: the cause was determined.

Similarly, in many normal contexts, questions concerning the behavior of S are appropriately answered in terms of (T), even though S is a mechanism. S's behavior is teleological in spite of the fact that it is being produced by a mechanism. "Why did S do that? (Why did the missile change course?)" is appropriately answered by "Because that will tend to bring about G (Because that will help it intercept the target-drone)," even though we know there is also an underlying mechanistic account. In this case, just as above, the underlying account is relevant to a further question concerning why S behaves according to this principle. But the possibility of a further question does not show that S *fails* to behave according to this principle. It explains, from one perspective, why it does.

And the argument that the underlying mechanistic account, as soon as it is found, simply supersedes the teleologicl characterization in every important context, just will not wash. For if, in response to the above question, I were to produce an elaborate mathematical story with a lot of electronic detail, my interrogator, if he understood me, might sarcastically reply, "You mean the missile tends to fly as the target—is that what you were trying to say?" In some contexts, the part of the story that goes beyond the simple teleological reply is irrelevant, obfuscatory and, hence, antiexplanatory. Further, it could easily be the case, for example, that a naval gunnery officer *has* to think of his homing missiles teleologically in order to best predict and control their behavior. It is possible that understanding them in any other way inhibits him. It is certainly the case that the operators of more mundane machinery are often better able to control it if they ignore much of the underlying mechanical detail. Racing drivers would probably be distracted to incapacity if they thought of what they were doing (while they were doing it) in terms of four-bar-linkages, rubber shear limits, and transient axial torques. So I take it that there is nothing in this very general argument against the possibility of a mechanism underlying purposive behavior.

Charles Taylor originally developed his precursor of (T) as an antimechanistic analysis. This in spite of the fact that he was well aware of the points and possibilities traced in the preceding paragraphs—and even sympathetic to most. To preserve the antimechanistic position in the face of these considerations, he invoked a subtle and attractive distinction that still has some currency.[21] I will conclude this chapter with an examination of that very important argument.

Taylor argues that indeed, it is obvious that (T) (or, rather, his version of it) applies to some behavior, for example, that of feedback devices, which has an underlying nonteleological account. But although this behavior is legitimately goal-directed, it is so only in a narrow, technical sense. Genuinely *purposive* behavior, that

---

21. This argument is offered in *The Explanation of Behavior*, pp. 20-24. He later softened on this position (see, e.g., his "Explaining Action," *Inquiry* 13:54-89, and his contribution to the anthology edited by R. Borger and F. Cioffe, *Explanation in the Behavioural Sciences* [Cambridge: Cambridge University Press, 1970]), but since it represents the best formulation of a rather tempting argument, it is worth pursuing in this form.

exhibited by man and the higher animals, however, is not so crudely *caused* by the circumstances: it is rather *elicited* by them. Accordingly, genuinely purposive behavior must result from inherent natural tendencies, which is to say, ones with no further, underlying explanation.

On this view the caused-versus-elicited distinction devolves upon the question of reducibility. Hence the whole sweep of our usual appreciation and explanation of animate behavior would have to be scrapped if it turns out that organisms are neurophysiological mechanisms. And since we have such an enormous panoply of support for the propriety of the ordinary, purposive sort of account, the plausibility, from this perspective, of supposing organisms to be intrinsic mechanisms of any sort is reduced to the vanishing point.

Perhaps Taylor's best statement of his position on this issue is one of his earliest.

the claim that 'the purposes' of a system are of such and such a kind affects the laws which hold at the most basic level. In other words, it [i.e., this claim] is incompatible with the view that the natural tendency towards a certain condition can itself be accounted for by other laws. Thus the function of an explanation invoking powers or natural tendencies can be precisely to shut off further enquiry. . . . Thus we could construct a mechanical dog, programmed to behave like a real one. In this case the laws descriptive of his external behavior [$y = f_1(x)$] would be teleological like those of his real counterpart, they would characterize the behavior as 'goal-directed,' but the more basic explanation [$y = f_2(x)$] would not. With systems of this kind we can hardly speak of an account in terms of 'natural' or 'inherent' tendencies.[22]

This statement is a particularly good one partly because it pointedly relates this argument to the position I have

22. *The Explanation of Behavior*, pp. 20-21.

been defending above, and also partly because it brings us back to the notion of natural tendencies with which we began. There is something compelling about the view that natural tendencies lie at the heart of teleology. But I also think that a misunderstanding of them lies at the heart of this view of mechanism.

The statement of a natural or normal tendency, according to this view,

> plays something of the kind of role in a teleological science of behavior that Inertia does, for instance, in Newtonian physics. In both cases the principles serve to make clear the kinds of event for which an antecedent must be adduced and the kinds of event for which this is not the case. For Newton's first Law, the continuation of a body at rest or in uniform rectilinear motion *did not admit* of explanation in this sense, only changes in velocity were to be accounted for. Continued rest or rectilinear motion could be spoken of in this sense as 'natural.' [Ibid., p. 23, italics mine]

So, similarly, teleological natural tendencies — purposes — do not admit of *any* further explanation, and *a fortiori*, not one in terms of a mechanism. From this it follows that any goal-directed behavior that is produced by a mechanism is not the exhibition of a natural tendency toward a goal at all. So animate behavior, behavior characterized and accounted for in terms of purpose, cannot be the product of an underlying, intrinsic mechanism.

The trouble with this argument is of course that incredible analysis of naturalness. The crucial observation here is that there are *other* examples of normalcy or naturalness which *do not* involve us in any very strong commitment to irreducibility, and these other examples are much closer relatives of the teleological one than is Newton's. Newton's first law 'did not admit of explanation' *only* within theoretical dynamics. Since the first law was a *presupposition* of the theory that seemed to make the most sense of dynamic phenomena, questioning it *within* the study of dynamics just could not, at that stage, be made sense of. But it is difficult to understand the notion of 'not admitting of explanation' outside of theoretical systematizations and their presuppositions. And the purposive explanations of animate behavior are not normally part of any systematic theory. In the more usual, more pedestrian, and much more analogous cases, natural tendency claims are not at all affected by underlying explainability. In the evolution of organisms, for example, there is a natural tendency for those structural features to survive which help the organism make its way against the elements. The fact that this tendency can be accounted for in terms of the nature of organic reproduction, inheritance of characteristics, and mutation, does not make it the least bit less natural. The case is similar for rocks that have a natural tendency to get hot when left sitting in the sun. This tendency would not be more natural if it did not have an underlying microphysical explanation. The irreducibility of purposive behavior and explanations simply cannot be supported in this way. There is nothing in the explanatory role of natural tendencies which supports the antimechanist thesis.

The drive to make animate natural tendencies irreducible to intrinsic-mechanistic regularities, at least in Taylor's case, results from a misperception of the distinction between 'accidental' and 'essential.' We understandably want to say that the goal-directedness of animal behavior is 'part of their essential nature' and does not 'just come about by accident.' And this is interpreted to mean that

the order or pattern which is visible in animate behaviour is radically different from that visible elsewhere in nature in that it is in some sense self-imposed; that the order is itself in some way a factor in its own production. This seems to be the force of the rejection of 'blind accident': the prevalence of order cannot be accounted for on principles which are only contingently or 'accidentally' connected with it, by laws whose operation only contingently results in it, but must be accounted for in terms of the order itself. . . .

The events productive of order in animate beings are to be explained not in terms of other unconnected antecedent conditions, but in terms of the very order which they produce. These events are held to occur because of what results from them, or, to put it in a more traditional way, they occur 'for the sake of' the state of affairs which follows. And this of course is part of what is meant by the term 'purpose' when it is invoked in explanation. [Ibid., p. 5]

The most interesting thing about this argument is that the feature of animate behavior Taylor wishes to hold out for here can be accommodated by (T) quite consistently with the mechanistic elaboration of it I have suggested above. One of the advantages of (T) over Taylor's formulation is that it explicitly shows teleological etiologies to be precisely those in which the consequences of the behavior to be accounted for play a role in bringing the behavior about. This is precisely what Taylor is driving at in the above passage when he speaks of the order being self-imposed. According to (T) it *is* "a factor in its own production," and we have already seen that this causal relationship is quite independent of an underlying mechanism.

As far as the accidental/essential issue is concerned, it really does not matter whether an organism's goal-directedness is at bottom irreducible or, alternatively, due to some *other* aspects of its makeup: either way it is a consequence of the organism's essential nature. It *is* its physiology. Furthermore, the only *worry* one could raise by invoking the accidental status of a property like the goal-directedness of behavior is an uncertainty about whether one could count on its persistence. And clearly *this* does not depend on irreducibility: intrinsic-mechanistic regularities are, after all, regularities.

It is possible that talking of 'reducibility' here is what misleads the antimechanists. Perhaps the terminology is inappropriately contentious. For it is difficult to speak univocally of the more *fundamental* account of the behavior of evolved organisms and designed feedback mechanisms. There is a perfectly good sense in which (in both cases) the teleological account is the most fundamental account — the underlying account — in *spite* of the fact that a mechanistic account is (or might be) also possible. In the case of consciously designed mechanisms, the teleological characterization of their behavior, something of the form (T), will be the design criterion. The explanation for there being any machine there at all, as well as much of its detail, is in terms of (T). The mechanism is explanatorily incidental. What we wanted was something (it did not really matter what) that would behave in a way that would tend to produce G, at least in certain circumstances. That the mechanism turned out to have certain *mechanical* details is interesting and explanatory only in certain narrowly circumscribed contexts: for example, where we are incredulous at its possibility, or where mechanical defects affect its performance. And even the notion of a defect makes sense only with respect to (T).

Exactly the same case can be made for organisms, but with natural selection replacing design. If it turns out that organisms are neurophysiological mechanisms that (sometimes) exhibit goal-directed behavior, and if their tendency to this particular behavior survived because of some selective advantage it provided, we can demote the details of the neurophysiological mechanism to the status of 'explanatorily incidental' in many contexts, just as with the consciously designed mechanisms above. For, once again, given the big (in this case, phylogenetic) picture, they behave like that precisely because that behavior satisfies (T). The goals, of course, are those that will help them stay alive and propagate.

Using the term 'reducibility' the way I have in this discussion may suggest that the intrinsic-mechanistic account is necessarily and unequivocally more explanatorily basic than the teleological account. And perhaps it is only *this* that antimechanists mean to deny in their resort to irreducible natural tendencies. This interpretation serves to make the explanatory basicness argument the central one, and for the run of normal mechanisms and organisms the same conclusion follows. For interpreted in this way, even if they are right, only non-designed machines and nonevolved organisms would be disqualified. And this also would break the link between animate behavior and the antimechanist thesis.

There is, finally, one more dramatic difficulty with the view that *irreducible* teleological behavior is the distinguishing feature of organisms, the ground for some special status or, perhaps, the hallmark of consciousness. If we accept either (T) or Taylor's formulation of it, or even Taylor's more idiomatic characterizations of teleology, it follows that the behavior of electrons in what is called 'Pauli interactions' is unquestionably teleological. Pauli's exclusion principle (the law governing this behavior) states that the electrons associated with any atom must array themselves among the permissible, discrete energy states such that no more than one electron occupies any energy state.[23] This establishes a *final* condition or result

23. It is often put in more straightforward quantum mechanical terms. Robert Kingsbury(*Elements of Physics* [New York: Van Nostrand-Reinhold, 1965], p. 528) puts it thus: "no two electrons in any atom may be represented by identical sets of

controlling the behavior of electrons in certain sorts of interaction. So the behavior of electrons is in these cases explained by appeal to the fact that it brings about that result. According to (T), or any of Taylor's formulations, this is just what it means to say behavior is teleological or goal-directed. Other bits of teleological terminology fit just as well: the electron did such-and-such *in order to* avoid occupying the same energy state as another electron. Thus Eric Rogers explains the repulsion of colliding atoms and the distortion of their respective electron "shells":

A modern physicist would point to Pauli's exclusion principle; in a collision the electrons of one atom *have* to steer clear of the electrons of the other, leaving the nuclei to repel.[24]

Presumably, the electrons have to do this *in order that* no two of them occupy the same energy state.

Now, I do not take this much to be very exciting. Goal-directedness, as represented by (T), is a scientifically respectable notion, with a straightforward empirical demonstration. So discovering a teleological phenomenon in physics should not be any cause for alarm. With a little imagination similar examples could no doubt be cooked up using conservation principles or the impossibility form of thermodynamic laws. These, however, would be less interesting simply because the prima facie teleological behavior would be so *palpably* the result of a conspiracy of intrinsic factors. In the case of a Pauli interaction, *all* we can say about one aspect of electron behavior is that a

---

quantum numbers." Gordon Stipe (*The Development of Physical Theories* [New York: McGraw-Hill, 1967], p. 401) offers a variation: "no two electrons in the same atom may have the same wave function."

24. *Physics for the Inquiring Mind* (Princeton, N.J.: Princeton University Press, 1960), p. 732.

certain result demands it. For all we know, Pauli's exclusion principle may be a bedrock law of nature. Clearly it is not impossible that it be so. The bare possibility of this, it seems to me, is enough to disqualify the irreducibility of teleological behavior from the demarcating function it is given in this argument.

FURTHER CONCLUSIONS

I think we may conclude from our examination of animate teleology that any argument against the neurophysiological explainability of organic behavior will have to come from within the current dispute raging over the explanatory role of human action concepts, which will be examined in chapter four. It also seems clear, however, that if one makes a more or less conventional distinction between men and animals, there is *nothing* in our ordinary appreciation of animal behavior inconsistent with the eventual neurophysiological explainability of that behavior.

Finally, and not altogether inadvertently, the foregoing discussion of the problem of mechanism provides further support for (T). The ability of this formulation to handle Taylor's philosophically exotic characterization of organic teleology substantially strengthens its claim to capture adequately what it is about behavior that is teleological.

CHAPTER III

FUNCTIONS

The consequence-etiologies of (T) represent what is paradigmatically teleological about characterizations (and hence explanations) of directed behavior in terms of goals. There is a sense in which invoking a consequence-etiology is just explaining behavior teleologically: the differences among conscious, animate, and mechanical cases can be viewed as mere matters of detail so far as the *form* of the account is concerned. The details are very important, of course, from a number of perspectives; that is what justifies devoting all of chapter four to them. But it is the consequence-etiological form that the paradigm and the metaphorically extended cases have in common. And since the metaphors are dead, we may say that having this sort of etiology is literally just what it is for behavior to be teleological. More generally, the consequence-etiology represents something important about teleology simpliciter, not just teleological explanations of behavior. Nearly everybody agrees that a certain forward orientation is what is characteristic of teleology in general, and it is *this* that is captured by the consequence-etiology.

In this chapter I will extend this powerful notion to cover the main group of teleological ascriptions and explanations not handled by (T): functions. The 'in order to' of functional ascriptions is a teleological 'in order to.' Its role in functional ascriptions (the heart beats in order to circulate blood) is quite parallel to the role of 'in order to' in goal ascriptions (the rabbit is running in order to escape from the dog). Accordingly, the formulation that results from this analytical exercise will bear an extremely intimate relation to (T). It will nevertheless be importantly distinct, and since this offends the spirit of much of the literature on the topic, the distinction deserves brief initial comment.

'Goal-directed' is a behavioral predicate. The *direction* is the direction of behavior. When we *do* speak of objects (homing missiles) or individuals (General MacArthur) as being goal-directed, we are speaking indirectly of their behavior. We would argue against the claim that they are goal directed by appeal to their behavior (e.g., the missile, or the General, did not change course at the appropriate time, and so forth). Conversely, many things have *functions* (e.g., chairs and windpipes) which do not behave *at all*, much less goal-directedly. And behavior can have a function without being goal-directed (e.g., pacing the floor or screaming out in pain). But even when goal-directed behavior has a function, very often its function is different from the achievement of its goal. For example, some fresh-water plankton diurnally vary their distance below the surface. The goal of this behavior is to keep light intensity in their environment relatively constant. This can be determined by experimenting with artificial light sources in the way suggested by (T). But the *function* of this behavior is to keep the oxygen supply constant, which normally varies with sunlight intensity. There are many instances to be found in the study of organisms in which the function of a certain goal-directed activity is not some further goal of that activity, as it usually is in human behavior, but is rather some natural concomitant or consequence of the immediate goal. Other examples are food-gathering, nest-making, and copulation. Clearly function and goal-directedness are not congruent concepts. There is an important sense in which they are wholly distinct. In any case, the relationship between functions and goals is a complicated and tenuous one, and becoming clearer about the nature of that relationship is one of the aims of this chapter.

The recent literature has been incautious in another way, too. The word 'function' and its derivatives function in a number of different ways, not all of which are clearly or closely related to teleology. I refer here not merely to mathematical functions and state functions, but to the verb 'to function' and the adjective 'functional' as well. It is not at all clear, for example, that I, myself, have any specific function; and yesterday morning I didn't even have anything to do. It is nonetheless appropriate to say that yesterday morning I simply could not function because I had a cold. Similarly, to explain how the heart functions (serial muscular contractions and such) is not to say what the function of the heart is; to note that an engine is functioning (or functional) is not to say anything about the functions it might serve. Some commentators have, I think, been led astray by a cavalier disregard for these grammatical nuances.[1] And since the focus of a teleologically oriented study must be the functions themselves which things have, or alternatively, are, I will for the most part use 'function' as a noun, with the verbs 'to have' and 'to be.' I will cleave to these formulations especially when I feel there is much danger of misunderstanding.

CONSCIOUS FUNCTIONS

The attributions of functions which I am taking as paradigmatic here, those underwritten by the presence of

---

1. See, e.g., W. Wimsatt, "Different Senses of 'Function' and the Concept of Teleology," *Studies in History and Philosophy of Science* 3:49, 50, and 51.

human intent, I will refer to as 'conscious functions.'
(These will be contrasted later with the 'natural functions' of organs, emergency reactions, protective devices,
and so forth, of organisms). The clearest cases of conscious functions involve artifacts that have been explicitly
designed to do something or other. The least ambiguity is
to be found in examples such as the function of the switch
on my office wall, the handle of an eggbeater, a watch's
sweep-second hand, or a headlight dimmer switch. We
can be most univocal in our reply when asked for the
function of things like the banking lever of a furnace, the
reset button on an electric appliance, or the tread of a
tire. Even if we do not know the answer (the function), we
have a good idea both how to find out and what would
count as getting the answer right. But these are only the
most central cases. As Richard Sorabji has pointed out,[2]
things can get functions of this sort as a result of conscious
effort, which falls considerably short of being full-fledged
design. We may feel more *comfortable* saying the function of the split hand of a stopwatch is to allow the timing
of immediately successive events on a single watch, but
there is nothing barbarous in saying the function of the
newspaper shoved under the door is to block a draft. And
the function of planting deciduous trees on the west side
is (sometimes) to provide shade in summer while allowing
sun in winter. In each of these (latter) cases it would be
unduly hyperbolic to characterize the thing with the
function as being *designed* to do what it does, although
we *would* naturally say it was there *by* design, which is
significantly different.

This last way of putting the matter takes us more than
halfway toward seeing the relation between functions and

2. "Function," *Philosophical Quarterly* 14:290.

consequence-etiologies; it also indicates something of the differences that will distinguish the function formulation from (T). As might be surmised from the list of cases above, the function of something, X, is always some consequence of X's being there (wherever) or of its having a certain form. And although 'there' sounds intolerably vague and difficult to the philosophical ear, it is, significantly, usually clear enough in a specific application. The paper is under the door, the tread is on the (periphery of the) tire, the dimmer switch is simply anywhere within easy reach. The function in each case is a consequence of those things being in those "places." The draft gets blocked, skids are avoided in the wet, and the headlight beam is able to be adjusted—all in virtue of those things being where they are. In some contexts it is more natural to talk of the consequence proceeding from the form of the artifact, rather than its place. Concerning the function of the split hand on the stopwatch mentioned previously, we might feel slightly easier characterizing that function as a consequence of the hand's having the particular form it does, rather than its just being there. It will be especially important to bear this in mind later when we discuss cases in which there is a multiplicity of functions. It is always possible, however, to formulate these cases, albeit sometimes awkwardly, in terms of 'being there,' properly understood: the function is a consequence of something with precisely that form being there. So for expository simplicity (it would be nearly impossible to read otherwise), I will adopt the 'being there' formulation, with the explicit understanding that it covers form as well as place.

Of course, not every consequence is a function. Some are merely inevitable (uninteresting) concomitants. Others, though pleasant enough (interesting), are merely happy accidents: and serendipity is distinguishable from function. One (inevitable, boring) consequence of the dimmer switch being where it is, is that the heel of my shoe occasionally catches on it; but surely this is not its function—or even one of many, if it has a number of them. And although it is indeed very *convenient* that the oil leaking from my car's engine keeps the grime washed off the timing mark, that is not the function of the oil leak: the leak *has* no function; I could not have it fixed if it did.

The etiological condition is what distinguishes consequences that are functions from those that are not. The function of X is that particular consequence of its being where it is which explains why it is there. The dimmer switch is there in virtue of one particular consequence: it allows adjustment of the headlight beam. The paper is jammed under the door because that has one consequence in particular: it blocks the draft. The sweep hand of my watch may keep the numbers free of dust, but that is not why it is there: so that is not its function. Its function is making seconds easier to read: *that* is the reason it is there. And this sense of 'in virtue of,' 'because,' 'why,' and 'reason' this notion of explanation, is plainly etiological. It concerns how the thing with the function came to be there (in the sense discussed), and this is precisely the sense given to 'etiological' in our previous analysis. This in turn shows what is wrong with characterizing the function of something merely as 'what it's good for.' Artifacts turn out to be good for all sorts of things that are not their functions. Dimmer switches are sometimes good for scratching your toe, sweep-second hands may keep the dust off the numerals, banking levers often make a good place to hang your hat. By contrast, the *function* of something is the *particular* thing that it is good for, which gives the proper insight into its etiology; it's what explains why it is there.

The distinction we are concerned with here is sometimes put in more classic terminology: it is the difference between X's function, on the one hand, and something X does only 'by accident,' on the other. The etiological analysis of function accounts for the propriety of this way of making the distinction. If the dimmer switch makes a particularly good foot scratcher, that is only an accident; that is not why it is there[3] and hence not its function. It is only happy chance if the banking lever makes a particularly good hat rack; it is the merest serendipity that the weep hand brushes dust off the marks on the watch face. So 'accidental' is an insightful way of characterizing what it is about these things which prevents them from being the functions of those artifacts.

Both the similarities and the differences between happy accidents and true functions are sometimes ingenuously marked by use of the expression 'function as.' We would naturally say that the dimmer switch can function *as* a foot scratcher; the banking lever sometimes functions *as* a hat rack; the sweep hand is functioning *as* a dust brush. But 'function as' is another expression to be wary of in this context. For it is importantly prototypical, anticipatory, attention-directing talk: it points to something that might well be a reason to create or place an artifact somewhere, and hence to a function we might *give* it.[4] But anticipation is valuably kept distinct from

3. Of course, if, in a particular case that *is* why it is there (Joe has an itchy clutch foot and bought one with a sharp top for just that reason — didn't even connect it to the headlight circuit), then foot scratching is its function in that case. But this is just the sort of exception that proves the rule: it passes precisely the test I am arguing must be passed. Foot scratching ability is only accidental in the normal, typical case. I will say more about the atypical cases below.

4. In the standard cases, what counts as giving something *another* function is fairly straightforward; e.g., giving the dimmer switch a special form or location in virtue of

attribution here. The sweep hand of my watch may function as a dust brush, but that is not its function. The Bible in the parson's pocket may have functioned as a bullet shield, but (unless we take seriously his story about supernatural intervention, which, again, *proves* the rule) that was not its function: that was not why it was there.

We might perhaps have suspected all this from the evident equivalence in this context of two superficially distinct types of interrogative sentence. 'What is the function of the vinyl cover on the playing field?' and 'Why is there a vinyl cover on the playing field?' both demand the same answer here: to keep the rain off. The ascription of a function simply *is* the answer to a 'Why?' question, and one with etiological force. If 'to keep the rain off' does not account for the cover's being there, if it is just something the cover is good for, like making puddles for the kids to play in, then it does not give the cover's function; neither does it answer the 'Why?' question. So not only do functional explanations provide consequence-etiologies, just like explanations in terms of goals, but the simple attribution of a function ipso facto *provides* that explanation (ascription-explanation), just as does the simple attribution of a goal to behavior. This displays the enormous parallel that obtains between goals and functions, and possibly accounts for the tendency in the philosophic literature to run them together. The *distinctions*, which have been hinted at, become clear only upon attempting a formulation for functions analogous to (T).

The formulation suggested by the considerations above is the following one.

---

convenience for foot scratching. However, some cases of giving something-which-already-exists a function, or another function, raise special problems that are treated later in this chapter under 'derivative cases.'

The function of X is Z iff:
>   (i) Z is a consequence (result) of X's being there,   (F)
>   (ii) X is there because it does (results in) Z

(Let me refer to this formulation as '(F).') The most significant difference between (F) and (T) concerns the consequence relation. One of the clearest, most central cases of goal-directedness we saw is trying-behavior, the *success* of which is not crucial to the ascription of a goal. This was directly responsible for the 'tends to' language in (T). The most central cases of functions, however, are all ones in which it can be said that X actually does (results in, has the consequence that) Z. Later we will discuss derivative cases of functions in which X cannot even be said to do Z, but these cases must be represented as derivative, not paradigmatic. Having pointed out this difference, it is important that it is not misunderstood. For, although in most cases there is no question at all about what it is for X to do Z, the matter is highly context-dependent. Thus it is worth noting that in some contexts X can be said to do Z even though Z never occurs. For example, the button on the dashboard activates the windshield washer system (that's what it does, I can tell by the circuit diagram) even though it never has and never will. All that seems required is that X be *able* to do Z under the appropriate conditions: in this case, when the button is pushed.

The other major difference of (F) from (T) is the use of the much more broadly ranging expression 'is there' in place of 'occurs.' As remarked above, 'is there' is a rather general place marker that takes on different significations in different sorts of cases, and in a way that is usually clear. We have seen some typical instances; other representative renderings are: 'exists (at all),' as in 'keeping snow from drifting across roads (and so forth) is why there are snow fences,' and 'Cs have them' as in 'headlights have parabolic reflectors because that concentrates all their light in one specific direction.' This latter case is one which could easily be put in terms of form: directional concentration of light is the reason headlight reflectors are *parabolic*. This difference (between (F) and (T)) is required by the fact that function-talk applies to a much broader range of things than goal-talk: namely to things other than behavior.

One further point should be made explicit before turning our attention to natural functions. In this discussion I have been taking the unique, definite article formulation of function ascriptions to be paradigmatic, in contrast to the indefinite article formulation. The cases I have examined have been primarily ones in which we naturally speak of *the* function of something, as opposed to *a* function, or *one* of its functions. Most treatments in the literature have taken these latter cases as their paradigms, probably in the interest of generality: 'a function' seems intrinsically more general than 'the function' since it avoids one obvious restriction. But this generality is superficial: the notion of a function is derivable from the notion of the function (more than one thing meets the criteria) just as easily as the reverse (only one thing meets the criteria). If more than one of X's consequences must be invoked to adequately explain why it is there, then (F) will have to nominate *both* of them as the function*s* of X. So as a matter of simple grammar, each will be *a* function of X. If the newspaper jammed under the door both blocks a draft and stops the door from rattling in the wind, and we could have achieved each of those ends in a number of independent ways, but chose this particular way *because* it did both at the same time, then (F) would require that we give functional status to both virtues. And indeed it is preanalytically clear in this case that the newspaper does have two functions. To omit either would be misrepresentation. So no difficulties arise from placing the analytic burden on the definite article formulation. And since the indefinite article formulation is more easily confused with the peripheral, proto-function, and nonfunction cases mentioned previously, using the unique cases is clearly the best strategy. The discussion here is only concerned with *a* function of X insofar as it is the sort of thing that would be *the* function of X if X had no others.

And, of course, to say that a functional explanation is adequate only if it mentions every function, is not to say that an adequate explanation provides a sufficient condition for the occurrence of X. As in chapter two, it is again worth explicitly pointing out that the ordinary, etiological notions of 'because' and 'reason' do not have the simple logical properties they are often taken to have. For example, if Z is the reason that Cs have Xs, it does not follow *either* that Z is sufficient for Cs to have Xs, or that Z is necessary in order that Cs have Xs. The reason that Cadillacs used to have fins was purely stylistic: they appealed to popular taste. But such appeal was not sufficient for Cadillacs to have fins: they might simply have been too expensive to tool up for. Nor was it necessary: they could have been there for aerodynamic reasons, irrespective of how they looked. Popular appeal was, nevertheless, the reason Cadillacs had fins. They were there because of that appeal. It is in this perfectly objective sense that function attributions are explanatory. And I think it is clear that pointing this out is enormously important in understanding the logic of functions, and not incidentally, teleological explanations as well.

NATURAL FUNCTIONS

The point of this chapter is to say something helpful
about function attributions and functional explanations
in instances not underwritten by human design or intent.
How are we to understand such claims as, 'the heart beats
in order to circulate blood,' or 'the function of a porcupine's coat of quills is to protect the little beast from
predators'?[5] Given a background of natural selection,
these cases — natural functions — can be understood in the
very same terms as conscious functions, namely in terms
of (F), with only the slightest change in nuance. For just
as conscious functions provide a consequence-etiology by
virtue of conscious selection, natural functions provide
the very same sort of etiology as a result of natural
selection.[6]

To make clear just how close the parallel here is, it is
important to say something first about the unqualified
notion of selection, from which natural selection is
derived. If we take the standard position that the paradigm cases of selection involve conscious choice, perhaps
even deliberation, then we can understand other uses of
'select' and 'selection' as extensions of this use. We can do
this by drawing attention to specific individual *features* of
the paradigm which occur in subconscious or noncon-
scious cases; and of course the range of extensions arrays

5. It is difficult to know in this connection just how best to handle the question of
supernatural design. Different theological positions seem to require different analytical strategies. But since the issue here is to determine what sense we can make of
function-talk in the absence of conscious effort, I have postponed all explicit theological considerations until later in the chapter. They can then be shown to fit in, in a way
which I think will be congenial to nearly every reflective position.
6. Wimsatt, "Different Senses of 'Function,'" has pointed out eloquently, and in
some detail, the intimate connection between teleological explanation and the notion
of selection. His more general remarks are, I think, rather off target, however, and
will be given further consideration below.

itself into a spectrum from more or less literal to openly metaphorical. There is, however, an important distinction within the paradigmatic, conscious cases. I can say I selected something, X, even though I cannot give a reason for having chosen it: I am asked to select a ball from among those on the table in front of me. I choose the blue one and am asked why I did. I may say something like, "I don't know, it just struck me I guess." Alternately, I could, without adding much, give something that has the form of a reason: "Because it's blue. Yes, I'm sure it was the color." In both of these cases I want to refer to the selection as 'mere discrimination,' for reasons that will become apparent. There are a number of contexts in which another, more elaborate reply is possible and natural. I could say something of the form, "I selected X because X does Z," where Z would be some possibility opened by X, some advantage that would accure from X, or some other result of having (using, etc.) X. "I chose American Airlines because its five-across seating allows me to stretch out." Or, "They selected DuPont Nomex because of the superior protection it affords in a fire."[7] Let me refer to selection by virtue of resultant advantage of this sort as 'consequence-selection.' Plainly, it is this kind of selection, as opposed to mere discrimination, that lies behind conscious functions: the consequence *is* the function. It is specifically this kind of selection of which *natural* selection represents an extension.

But the parallel between natural selection and conscious consequence-selection is much more striking than is sometimes thought. True, the presence or absence of

7. Of course the advantage is not always stated explicitly; "I chose American because of its five-across seating." But for it to be selection of the sort described here, as opposed to mere discrimination, something like an advantage must be at least implicit.

volition is an important difference, at least in some contexts. We might want to say that *natural* selection is really *self*-selection, that nothing is *doing* the selecting; given the nature of X, Z, and the environment, X will *automatically* be selected. Quite so. But here the above distinction between kinds of conscious selection becomes crucial. For consequence selection, by contrast with mere discrimination, deemphasizes volition in just such a way as to blur its distinction from natural selection on precisely this point. In the conscious cases, the consequences are selection *criteria*. So we can say in these cases too that given X, Z, and the environment, which includes the selection criteria, X will be selected automatically in just the same way.[8] The cases are very close indeed.

The parallel has been drawn in a slightly different fashion by Francisco Ayala,[9] a geneticist.

Natural selection has been compared to a sieve which retains the rarely arising useful and lets go the more frequently arising harmful mutants. Natural selection acts in that way, but it is much more than a purely negative process, for it is able to generate novelty by increasing the probability of otherwise extremely improbable genetic combinations. Natural selection is creative in a way. It does not "create" the genetic entities upon which it operates, but it produces adaptive genetic combinations which would not have existed otherwise. The creative role of natural selection must not be understood in the sense of the "absolute" creation that traditional Christian theology predicates of the Divine act by which the universe was brought into being *ex nihilo*. Natural selection may be compared rather to a painter which creates a picture by mixing and distributing pigments in various ways over the canvas. The canvas and the pigments are not created by the artist but the painting is. It is conceivable that a random combination of the pigments might result in the orderly whole

8. This is another manifestation of the classic tension between rationality and freedom.
9. "Teleological Explanations in Evolutionary Biology," *Philosophy of Science* 37:5.

which is the final work of art. Some modern paintings look very much like a random association of materials, to be sure. But the probability of, say, Leonardo's *Mona Lisa* resulting from a random combination of pigments is nearly infinitely small. In the same way, the combination of genetic units which carries the hereditary information responsible for the formation of the vertebrate eye could have never been produced by a random process like mutation. Not even if we allow for the three billion years plus during which life has existed on earth. The complicated anatomy of the eye like the exact functioning of the kidney are the result of a nonrandom process — natural selection.

The worry about the traditional Christian notion of creation ex nihilo is of course wholly gratuitous for our purposes here. Human creations are not ex nihilo either, and that is the parallel I wish to establish.[10] From an etiological point of view, it should be clear how difficult, not to say obscurantist, it is to drive much of a conceptual wedge between conscious and natural consequence-selection.

There is one further feature of (F) which must be given a special emphasis vis-a-vis natural functions. Much of B. F. Skinner's objection, expressed in chapter one, to talk of what I am calling natural functions stems from an evidently misleading grammatical feature of (F). Skinner seems to think that to say the spider possesses its web-making ability because that helps it to catch food, as (F) requires, involves us in untenable reference to a specific spider's future food catching. This would, of course, offend the actual (i.e., evolutionary) etiological picture:

10. Relatedly, one of the difficulties that usually plages discussions of Divine creation is the invocation of a notion of creation with which nobody has any experience; this allows the logical bamboozling which often characterizes its role in these discussions. It is both entertaining and enlightening to try seriously to describe fairly pedestrian cases in which it is reasonable to talk of creation out of nothing whatever, and to make clear sense of attributing that act of creation to somebody in particular.

the fly just consumed by Horatio the spider was not in any way involved in the etiology of Horatio's web-spinning ability. But in fact, this reference can be avoided, and this is worth pointing out in some detail.

First of all, when we say 'the spider (or, a spider) possesses the ability to spin a web because that allows it to catch food,' 'the' and 'a' are seldom used to refer to a specific individual, and 'that' *never* does. 'The spider' is usually equivalent to 'spiders' (like, 'the American farmer') and 'that' invariably refers to a property (e.g., an ability or propensity) of a certain *type* of thing, and logically cannot be limited to a specific instance of the type. To make this explicit, the sentence above might be rendered, 'spiders possess the ability to spin webs because web-spinning helps catch food.' But even in the unusual case in which we are called upon to express the etiology of a particular spider's ability to spin a web, the operative property term must remain general, and (in a sense) abstract: Horatio has the capacity to spin a web because web-spinning helps catch food. So in the standard formulation, 'X is there because it does Z,' it is important to recognize that there is a sense in which X *may* refer to a specific instance (spider or kidney), but Z may not. Furthermore, the pronoun 'it' (in 'it does Z') is misleading in the individual case in a way it is not when talking of entire classes.

This grammatical caution has an important but incomplete parallel in conscious cases. We do not want to say the actual banking of my furnace last night — that specific instance of banking — was itself necessarily involved in the etiology of the banking lever. Nevertheless, we want to say the lever (that particular lever) is there because it does that. So once again we must warn that the 'that' here does not refer to a particular banking by a particular lever, but rather to the general banking ability of banking levers. The parallel is not complete because conscious selection can take place with respect to a specific instance and does not require generations as does natural selection. If this particular lever doesn't work, then we can (will!) get a new one. Consequently, the 'it' in 'X is there because it does " is less likely to be misleading in these cases. I think this is the major structural difference between conscious and natural functions, and it is on this consideration that any talk of a difference in kind between the two must rest. Obviously there is *some* difference. If this analysis is right, it consists merely in the typicality of generations. And since generation-talk is clearly appropriate in the case of some conscious functions (assembly line production of some simple units), and repair of all sorts (both surgical and other) is possible for natural malfunctions, the distinction is not sharp even here.

The second aspect of Skinner's objection is a worry about verb tenses. Why not put the etiological contention in the past tense and avoid the problem altogehter? Why not say X is there because in the past Xs have done Z? The reason is twofold and very important. First, use of the past tense in this way blurs the distinction between functional and vestigial organs, which is worth some pains to avoid in this context. Both kidneys and appendixes are there because of the function they had in the past; only kidneys are there because they do what they do, which is to say only kidneys (still) have a function. In general, when we explain something by appeal to a causal principle, the tense of the operative verb is determined by whether or not the principle itself holds at the time the explanation is given. Whether the causally relevant events are current or past is irrelevant. To put it any *other* way would be misleading. We might say, for example, "The *Titanic* sank because when you tear a hole that size in the bow of a ship it sinks," using the verb 'to sink' in the present tense even though the sinking in question took place in the past. *When* the sinking took place is just not relevant to the appropriate tense of the verb. And nobody is misled by the tense of the verb into thinking that the *Titanic* is just now sinking. If we were to throw the statement into the past tense it would imply that nowadays one could get away with tearing a hole that size in the bow of a ship without it sinking. If I were to use the past tense merely because the causally relevant event took place in the past, *that* would be misleading. So changing the tenses around is not the answer; this is how the vestigial/functional confusion arises. A little logical caution is the better remedy.

Furthermore, as hinted above, exactly the same grammatical convolution is found in the conscious cases, which shows from yet another perspective how closely wedded the two sorts of function are. For on Skinner's grounds we might be urged to say, for example, the dimmer switch is there not because it allows us to adjust the headlights, but rather because in the past it and/or others were effective in adjusting the headlights. And precisely the same criticism applies. If we take seriously the above caution to construe Z as the general property of a class (or, at least a potential class), no difficulty arises: the etiology is clear and the functional insight preserved. 'It's there because it does that' is in a sense shorthand for, 'it's there because things like it in the appropriate way have that sort of property.' But even for clarity, the shorthand is usually preferable: we simply are not misled in the way Skinner expects us to be.

The major ambiguities and difficulties in applying (F) to natural functions should now have been removed.

Some illustrations will test (and firm) our understanding. The function of chlorophyll is to enable plants to undergo photosynthesis. This squares with (F) i, because enabling plants to undergo photosynthesis *is* a consequence of chlorophyll's being there; and it squares with (F) ii, since, on the evolutionary account, that is precisely why it has survived in the birth-decay cycle: that is why it is there. Similarly for the porcupine's spines: protection is a consequence of their being there, and that is clearly why things with spines, and hence the spines themselves, have survived. Vestigial cases have already been treated: whatever they did is no longer a consequence of their being there, hence they have no function. The bilateral symmetry of most organisms, while not vestigial, also has no function; and this too squares with (F), because it can not be accounted for by appeal to any of its consequences: it is there only as the result of embryonic cell division.[11]

Of course, if we give (F) this interpretation it must be clear that the 'because' (and hence 'reason,' 'why,' 'in virtue of,' etc.) is independent of the philosophical reasons/causes distinction. But this should have been expected since the (deliberate) reason of conscious functions is etiological in precisely the sense relevant here: it offers an account of how the thing came to be there, or have the form it does. Functions of both kinds offer consequence-etiologies, and do so as ascription-explanations: merely ascribing a function is to offer a consequence etiological account of the existence or form of the thing with the function. So functions share the two logical properties characteristic of teleology. Function attributions are teleological explanations.

---

11. But as Wimsatt has pointed out "Different Senses of 'Function,'" sometimes *lack* of bilateral symmetry has a function: e.g., in the case of flounders.

The close parallel I am insisting on here between conscious and natural functions is supported by three further considerations. First of all, just as before, several superficially different requests seem to be requests for the same thing. 'Why do porcupines have a coat of quills?,' 'What are the quills there for?' and 'What is the function of the quills?' are all answered by 'To protect the wretched little beast from hungry predators.' The function is what it's there for. And 'What's it there for?' is a request for the reason it is there. That is, it is equivalent to 'Why do porcupines have such a coat?' 'Why is it there?' is not asking merely 'What's it *good for*?' It is good for all sorts of things that are not 'What it's there *for*': sleeping on, avoiding certain irritants, perhaps even tooth-picking. But none of these things is what the coat is *there* for, none is the function of the coat. The spines only do those things by accident if they do them at all. The function of the coat is that particular thing it's good for which explains why it's there.

It seems clear that only an etiological analysis can make the required sense of the function/nonfunction distinction in cases like this. And the importance of this distinction for natural function attributions can be seen by noticing that it functions in evolutionary biology just as we should expect if this use is derived directly from the conscious paradigms.

I remember a particularly relevant oral discussion of the function of inquilinism among pearlfishes. These slender-bodied fishes live in the respiratory systems of sea cucumbers. They apparently emerge at night to forage, and return at dawn to their hosts. They are largely without pigment, and there is some evidence that they are harmed by exposure to daylight. The question arose: Do these fishes enter the sea cucumbers to avoid light, or do they do so to avoid predators? The feeling of the group seemed to be that if the behavior fulfills both needs, it must be regarded as having a dual function. This is a physiologically valid conclusion, but teleonomically naive.... The habit of entering holothurians developed as a defense against predators, and the fish became extremely specialized in behavior and physiology for exploiting the advantages of inquilinism. This required or permitted the degeneration of a number of adaptations: the caudal fin disappeared; the eyes were reduced; and the integumentary pigments and other defenses against light were reduced in effectiveness.[12]

So the function is defense against predators, not against light. Once again, just as we found with E. S. Russell in the last chapter, we find a serious scientist making important and subtle distinctions by deploying this teleological concept in the etiological way required by our analysis. Once again we have an example in which two candidates for attribution (in this case, of functionhood) seem prima facie equally deserving, but are distinguished on the basis of etiological considerations, and precisely those suggested by (F). We also find here several different locutions of the sort discussed above being used interchangeably in an overwhelmingly plausible manner.

Finally, the third consideration I wish to adduce explicitly in endorsement of a very tight relationship between conscious and natural functions is the parallel in the case of multiple functions. The liver, for example, has several functions: secretion of bile, conversion of sugars, production of urea, and perhaps others. According to (F), this means that each of those activities must be mentioned in an adequate evolutionary account of why animals that have livers have them. And the argument offered by Williams above suggests that is precisely what evolutionary biologists would say. What the claim to multiple

---

12. This quotation is from George C. Williams, *Adaptation and Natural Selection* (Princeton, N.J.: Princeton University Press, 1966), pp. 266-267.

functions *cannot* mean, as we have seen, is that the liver is merely *good for* doing all those things: that would obliterate the function/accident distinction, which is so crucial to conceptualizations in these terms. Even livers are good for things that are not their functions: lunch (with onions) for instance.

ISSUES AND TRENDS IN THE
CURRENT LITERATURE

The analysis of the concept of function presented here grew out of a critical reflection on a series of articles which appeared in the 1960s. These were the papers (in chronological order) by Hempel,[13] Canfield,[14] Sorabji,[15] Lehman,[16] Gruner,[17] and Beckner[18] — all of which offer an analysis of function in roughly the same spirit as this chapter. An earlier analysis by Beckner[19] also influenced the reasoning that led up to this chapter. Beckner's two analyses are markedly different, so let me for convenience refer to them respectively as Beckner[I] and Beckner[II], in chronological order (the book first, then the article). Since the analysis of this chapter was developed, three more important analyses have appeared by Ayala,[20] Ruse,[21] and Wimsatt.[22] These ten analyses share an over-

13. "The Logic of Functional Analyses," *in Symposium on Sociological Theory*, ed. L. Gross (New York: Harper & Row, 1959).

14. "Teleological Explanations in Biology," *The British Journal for the Philosophy of Science* 14:285-295.

15. "Function," pp. 289-302.

16. "Functional Explanations in Biology," *Philosophy of Science* 32:1-20.

17. "Teleological and Functional Explanations," *Mind* 75:516-526.

18. "Function and Teleology," *Journal of the History of Biology* 2:151-169.

19. *The Biological Way of Thought* (Berkeley and Los Angeles: University of California Press, 1968).

20. "Teleological Explanations," pp. 1-15.

21. "Function Statements in Biology," *Philosophy of Science, 38,* 87-95.

22. "Different Senses of Function," pp. 1-80.

lapping cluster of difficulties that may be treated with some economy from the perspective developed here. This treatment will, I think, show the analysis embodied in (F) to represent some improvement on the current literature; it seems to capture the requisite insights, but at the expense of none of the central difficulties that have always accompanied those insights.

One with similar sympathies

With the exception of Ayala, none of these authors offers an etiological account, and hence, with that exception, none can handle the fine-structure of functional conceptualizations which depends upon an etiological rendering. There are many aspects of Ayala's analysis that are strikingly close to contentions I have been at pains to establish here, specifically, a function/accident distinction, and a conceptual unification of conscious and natural functions. In fact, a major difficulty in Ayala's analysis is an assimilation of the various forms of teleology which is too complete. His conflation of functions with goals leads him to insist that for function-talk to be appropriate, the system under consideration must be directively organized (p. 12). And, as we have seen, distinguishing between functions and goal-directedness is an essential part of understanding teleological conceptualizations, especially when they apply simultaneously (which, of course, is not always the case). Furthermore, this same conflation leads Ayala to ascribe an 'ultimate' goal or purpose to natural selection itself: reproductive efficiency (p. 10). Wimsatt has a less tractable form of the same problem: his analysis seems to *require* the explicit purposefulness of evolution. Either way this is a problem. For the sense in which evolution itself is goal-directed is something that needs examination and support, it cannot be simply presupposed. For if this way of speaking *does* make sense, it is importantly different sense from that of the comparatively straight-forward examples discussed in chapter two. One would guess that it will turn out to be metaphorical in a differ-ent and less mortal sense than those cases. It seems much better merely to hold that natural selection, including all the detail concerning inheritance of characteristics, reproduction, and survival, is the sort of principle that underwrites consequence-etiological explanations: this much it surely does. By doing this we can say that it 'functions *as*' a purpose; but we need not take the gratui-tous risk involved in the unqualified assertion that it *is* purposeful.

The second problem in Ayala's account arises from the fact that he fails to see that consequence-etiologies are the hallmark of teleology. He probably does not see that his analysis invokes a single *type* of etiology at all: he never explicitly mentions the point in these terms. In any case, casting about for a plausible way to characterize the dis-tinction between teleological systems and nonteleological ones he falls on the notion of utility. "I suggest the use of the criterion of utility to determine whether an entity is teleological or not" (p. 12). In the conscious cases, this leads him to an implausible and ad hoc construction of utility merely to avoid obvious counterexamples. With respect to the natural cases, however, the consequences of this move are even more serious, for he defines 'utility' in living organisms by "reference to survival or reproduc-tion. A structure or process of an organism is teleological if it contributes to the reproductive efficiency of the organism itself, and if such contribution accounts for the existence of the structure or process" (p. 13). And this seems to suggest that it is impossible by the very nature of the concepts—logically impossible—that organismic structures and processes get their functions by the conscious intervention (design) of a Divine Creator. This, I think, is an analytical arrogance. I am, personally, certain that the evolutionary account is the correct one. But I do not think this can be determined by conceptual analysis: it is not a matter of logic.

If Ayala had noticed that his analysis already contained an adequate teleological/nonteleological distinction, had he noticed that the notion of utility was an unnecessary addition, he would have avoided this unfortunate implication. For if the consequence-etiological rendering of functions is taken seriously, then both natural and conscious functions are functions by virtue of their being the reason the thing with the function 'is there,' subject to the restrictions we have discussed. The differentiating feature is merely the *sort* of reason appropriate in either case; specifically, whether a conscious agent was involved or not. But in the functional-explanatory context we are examining, the difference is minimal. When we explain the presence or existence of X by appeal to a consequence Z, the overriding consideration is that Z must be or create conditions conducive to the existence of X. The exact *nature* of the conditions is inessential to the possibility of this form of explanation: it can be looked upon as a matter of mere etiological detail. It is nothing in the essential form of the explanation. In *any* given case something could conceivably get a function through either sort of consideration. Accordingly, the consequence-etiological analysis begs no theological questions: the organs of organisms logically could get their functions through God's conscious design; but we can also make perfectly good sense of their functions in the absence of divine intervention. And in either case they would be functions in precisely the same sense. This of course was only accomplished by disallowing explicit mention of intent or purpose in accounting for conscious functions. Once again, the metaphor has died; and the logical form of the teleological conception is independent of the original paradigm.

Explanation

Although there are profound insights scattered throughout the other nine analyses, each one has far more difficulty squaring with the desiderata developed in this chapter than the one we have just examined. A major failing of nearly all these analyses concerns explanatoriness, and the failing takes three distinct forms. One position (taken by Gruner, Wimsatt, and possibly Ruse) is that functional explanations are indeed etiological, but are only contingently and only sometimes linked to function *ascriptions*. A second position (taken by Canfield, Lehman, and for some cases Sorabji) is that functional ascriptions are explanatory, but the explanation offered is not etiological. The third view (that of Hempel and Beckner[1]) is simply that functional attributions themselves are never explanatory.

The first of these positions looks relatively congenial to the view advanced in this chapter, but the difference actually is of crucial importance. For it amounts to abandoning the function/accident distinction, which we have seen is central to making sense of several useful points of function-talk. Nevertheless, one further example, pirated from another context,[23] might serve here to underline the

---

23. See my discussion of Ruse's paper "A Comment on Ruse's Analysis of Function Statements," *Philosophy of Science* 39:512-514.

centrality of this distinction. Consider someone with an anomalous condition (congenital defect) in which his stomach and lower bowel touch and share a wall in one spot: they are connected, but not interconnected; where the stomach and bowel are naturally close to one another, they have become as it were "welded" together, rather like a postoperative adhesion. Now if, per accidens, this person were to have an ulcer perforate at the point of attachment, the food and septic matter would be fortuitously discharged directly into the lower tract. This would certainly be painful, and treatment would clearly be called for; but the consequences would not be nearly so grave as they would have been if the contents of the stomach had drained directly into the abdominal cavity. In this latter case the resulting infection is nearly always fatal. So we could say that adhesion functioned *as* protection for the abdominal cavity against the perforation of this ulcer. But no one would say that was the *function* of the adhesion; it *has* no function: it is only there by accident. The case is exactly like the parson's Bible. Nevertheless, it behaves exactly like many cases of legitimate functions. Many emergency reactions and protective structures have the essential characteristics of this one: they would be merely fortuitous if it were not for their etiology. And, as far as I can see, the adhesion would have the protective function according to the analyses of those who take the position being criticized here: the *only* thing this case lacks is the appropriate etiology.

It is interesting to note that if people were particularly prone to ulcers in just the spot that our friend had the intestinal adhesion, and his anomalous condition were hereditary, it is possible that a race of people could evolve with precisely that bowel attachment. In the process the attachment would *get* the function of protecting the abdominal cavity from the perforation of a certain sort of ulcer. This is precisely how certain secretions which are only rarely useful got their functions. And this accords perfectly with the analysis embodied in (F).

We have already elaborately discussed the difficulties with the second of these positions. This is the view that the functional 'Why?' merely asks what the thing is good for, and merely constitutes another, and less defensible, way of abolishing the function/accident distinction.

It is the third position which has the most interesting philosophical implications. On page 112 of *The Biological Way of Thought*, Beckner contends that attributions of function ought to be denied the title of 'explanation.' Statements like, 'the function of chlorophyll in plants is to enable plants to perform photosynthesis,' are not, he contends, really explanatory.

For notice that nothing corresponding to an explanans and explanandum are distinguishable within the statement. Only the most Palaeozoic reactionary would maintain that "Plants have chlorophyll" is explained by "Plants perform photosynthesis." In any case, there is nothing in the statement that remotely resembles explanation in the Humean Pattern.

But reactionary or not, we have seen that there is a perfectly objective sense in which 'plants ave chlorophyll' is explained functionally by pointing out the role chlorophyll plays in enabling 'plants to perform photosynthesis': it answers a 'Why?' question by providing a perfectly respectable etiology; it provides the reason chlorophyll is there. And if the Humean Pattern cannot accommodate this sort of explanation, so much the worse for that pattern: it's no good trying to cover up inadequacies in the philosophical analysis of explanation by hurling political shibboleths.

Moreover, if anything is to count as Palaeozoic reaction here it has got to be the attempt to force legitimate functional explanation into the deductive model: trying to reformulate them as arguments for the conclusion that the thing with the function actually does exist. For the best looking argument of this sort, which has plausible premises, is (for the photosynthesis example):

A) Some plants survive because photosynthesis takes place within them.

B) Chlorophyll is the only substance which enables plants to perform photosynthesis.

Therefore: Some plants contain chlorophyll.

But there are two virtually insurmountable objections to this as a reconstruction of the functional explanation under consideration. In the first place, the functional explanation depends essentially on a selection background, whereas the above deduction does not. The first photosynthetic mutation would be amenable to a functional explanation on this deductive reconstruction, and we have already seen this to be conceptual nonsense. Second, the functional explanation could still be true, and explanatory, if B) were false. All that is necessary is that the chlorophyll actually perform photosynthesis, not that nothing else could have performed it.

It is precisely at this point, after attempting a reconstruction of just the sort we are considering here, that Hempel raises the haunting specter that frightened Taylor into this same analytical incaution: if there is nothing in the explanation itself which rules out all alternatives to the thing being explained (in this case the occurrence of chlorophyll) then can we legitimately say we have explained why specifically *IT* occurred, as opposed to something else? Phrasing the question in this way has led many good philosophers into the cul-de-sac we are presently exploring. For it imports an impossible version of the wrong sort of contrast into the explanatory inquiry. 'Why?' questions do indeed derive much of their sense from contrasts implicit in the context of inquiry; the perplexity being expressed is very often not clear until we understand something about what the person asking the question expected in the circumstances. But there are many such contrasts, not just one, and the contrast is virtually *never* the one suggested by the deductive requirement. For when the question 'Why P?' is readable as 'Why P, as opposed to something else?' the alternatives are usually finite and relatively easy to specify. For example, 'Why did you get a Ford?' might be asked in a context in which the contrast is obviously, '. . . as opposed to a Chevy or Plymouth?.' In this case, all that is required of an answer is that it differentiate buying a Ford from buying the other two. It need not justify buying a car in the first place; and not buying a car at all is one sort of alternative to buying a Ford. 'Why did *that* window break?' (The emphasis tells you when alternatives like this are the contrast.) 'That was the one that got stressed in mounting.' A *specific* contrast is all that must be made, not a general one with all possible alternative states of affairs. As far as I can see, nothing we can say will rule out *all* possible alternatives in a nontrivial way: in practical cases, physically sufficient conditions are simply impossible to state.

What tempts us to think a general contrast is being made is that in some cases there are no specifiable alternatives: we are simply incredulous that P happened at all. "Why did that window *break*?" suggests, "as opposed to *not* break?" But in these cases, the contrast is not general in the sense required by the deductive model. Changing the emphasis in this way does not shift the contrast from specific to general. Rather, it shifts the focus from instrumental causes to instigational ones. With the earlier emphasis the instigational cause was presumed (e.g., the window had been slammed, dropped, sonic-boomed, or otherwise maltreated) and the puzzle concerned instrumental considerations, differences among the panes. With the shift, that presumption is brought into question; but to answer the question, to provide an instigational cause, to explain why the window broke, to resolve *this* particular issue, does not require a sufficient condition for breaking windows — or even for breaking this window. All that is required is a plausible account of it: something to remove the incredulity. ("It was the sonic boom you heard just before it shattered.") For in this context, to find *an* account, is automatically to find the best account: the very question itself implies this. Even in the atypical case in which we find several plausible accounts, choosing among them by the standard investigative techniques does not (fortunately!) involve us in the specification of a sufficient condition: we simply find details of the circumstances surrounding the phenomenon which one or the other of the competing hypotheses cannot plausibly account for. We can in this way get the very best reason to suppose that the account we have offered is true, and hence, in some circumstances, we can have the very best reason to suppose that there *were* sufficient conditions present. But none of this requires that we know what those conditions were: the cause has been determined; we understand why it happened.

It was something like this that Dray was groping for when he termed answers to some such questions 'How possibly?' explanations.[24] This is, in a way, a misleading characterization; for not just *any* plausible account will do: we want the right *one*. So these are better represented as simply 'How?' explanations, or perhaps 'How actually?' explanations, in a context of incredulity. A large class of casual causal inquiries consist of 'Why?' questions in such a context: 'Why did the train crash?' 'Why did the house burn?' 'Why did Johnny come down with the measles?' There is no *specific* alternative to contrast these cases with, but that does not (fortunately!) imply a contrast with *all* alternatives. What these questions principally require is some intelligible way of avoiding the null hypothesis; and this our normal causal answers provide: bent rail, spontaneous combustion, exposure to Jimmy. And that philosophers have not yet provided a general account of cause, clearly displaying its relation to chance, does not provide the least reason to suspect these answers are fraudulent. If functional explanations are like these, they are as good as explanations ever get.

This brings us, finally, to the contention of Greulach and Adams that the teleological "explanation" does not explain, is not the explanation of, stomatal behavior. To disallow teleological (here: functional) explanation in this case is to fail to see that more than one perplexity is expressible by 'Why do the stomata open and close just as they do?' in this context. And treating the one Greulach and Adams do, actually sharpens another. For the long photochemical story merely provides the mechanism of stomatal behavior as a fait accompli. And as interesting

24. *Laws and Explanation in History* (London: Oxford University Press, 1957), pp. 158 ff.

as this mechanical story is, it serves to make Paley's incredulity more urgent: are we to suppose that this wondrously complicated and enormously useful mechanism occurred here merely by chance? Is this merely fortuitous, or is the mechanism there precisely because it does what it does? To deny the propriety of teleological explanation here is to deny the obviously right answer to this question: namely, that it is there because of its (otherwise inexplicably fortuitous) consequences.

The analysis presented in this chapter shows the teleological account required here to be the boringly orthodox one it is. And by the way, it provides an insight into Paley's mistake. Perhaps design does require a designer, that is a point we need not settle. For we have seen that the requisite teleological account can derive from a background of mere *selection*. Selection, either conscious or natural, can quiet the strident disbelief and set loose fortune's hostages. And, as we have also seen, selection does not require a selector. To suppose it does is the converse of the arrogance imputed to Ayala: neither supposition is cogent, although each is tempting in its way.

So there is a sense in which the functional account is better than either the theological account or the evolutionary one: for it is true on both. Settling the further issue is an independent empirical matter.

Natural versus conscious

Most of the authors being discussed here are content to divorce conscious functions from natural ones (Ayala, Beckner[II], and Wimsatt are the exceptions). Most philosophers writing on the subject have seen that natural functions are the most interesting and most problematic, and have focused all their attention on those cases, scarcely glancing at the conscious cases for help in developing their formulations. Consequently, these formulations are nearly impossible to apply to the conscious cases, no matter how well they accommodate the organs of organisms. But the fundamental lesson of this entire discussion is that the logical structure of natural functions is best understood by noticing its intricate parallels with conscious functions: by seeing that structure as issuing from the death of an explanatorily rich metaphor. And this result should not have been unexpected. Functional ascriptions of either sort have a profoundly similar ring. Compare, 'the function of that cover is to keep the distributor dry,' with, 'the function of the epiglottis is to keep food out of the windpipe.' It is even more difficult to detect a difference in what is being requested: 'What is the function of the human windpipe?' vs. 'What is the function of a car's exhaust pipe?' No analysis should begin by supposing that the two sorts are wildly different. That is a possible *conclusion* of an analysis, not a reasonable presupposition. Any analysis that can accommodate them both as functions in the same sense automatically has a point in its favor; any analysis that cannot has a difficulty it must explain away.

Systems

It is interesting that there is an element to be found in every analysis except Sorabji's which results directly from the general preoccupation with natural functions, and which also provides the single most serious obstacle to extending those analyses to cover the conscious cases. This is the essential relativization of each of those formulations to some system S, in which the thing with the function must be functioning. For the natural functions of organs and other parts of organisms, the system S is typically a natural unit, easy to subdivide from the environment: the organism itself. But for the conscious functions of artifacts, such systems must often be hacked out of the environment rather arbitrarily; and this makes the purport of the analyses difficult to see in these cases. It is just not clear in what system the newspaper jammed under the door is functioning. The tire tread example presents the same problem, allows some choice. But even in cases allowing unambiguous determination of the system in which the thing with the function is functioning, that system usually fails to be enough like an organism to fit a formula derived from evolutionary cases.

The nonetiological analyses are practically forced to this troublesome relativization. For if we ignore the requisite explanatory consideration, then utility seems to be the central feature of function-talk: that seems to be *the* common feature. But utility must be *to* something; ergo the system S. It is the appeal to utility which is directly responsible for the baroque character of many recent analyses (especially Beckner[II] and Wimsatt). If utility is conceived not in etiological terms, but rather in terms of the contribution something makes to the operation of a system, then intricate complexity is the natural result of trying to avoid accident counterexamples. But all these moves are futile, because the function/accident distinction *is* an etiological distinction. No matter what systematic requirement is proffered, an accident counterexample like the intestinal-adhesion case can be raised against it.

Yet even if needlessly baroque and ultimately futile, utility analyses that tie utility to a systematic contribution have many fewer problems than those that, seeing the relevance of natural selection, tie it directly to fecundity.

For this move makes it virtually impossible to include the conscious functions of artifacts; and withal, it does not even avoid the adhesion counterexample. Furthermore, it embraces an even more disastrous case, that paradigm of nonfunction: the heart's throb. For, as Frankfurt and Poole[25] pointed out years ago in a comment on Canfield's analysis, the noise of the heart has (survival and hence) fecundity value through its role as a diagnostic aid in detecting pathological conditions.

Utility to the System S clearly is not the answer.

Levels of Inquiry

As hinted at the end of the explanatoriness discussion above, one of the advantages of functional explanations is that they can often be given before a complete, deterministic theory of the subject matter in question is elaborated. Further, they are consistent with a variety of different elaborations. In this they are rather like the general notion of causal explanation in terms of which they have been analyzed here: causes can be objectively determined without knowing much about the exact structure of causal laws governing the phenomenon. Hertz had *established* the causal role of ultraviolet light in his photoelectric effect experiment long before the theoretical analysis of that effect was elaborated. In fact, establishing that role provided invaluable data in the search for a theoretic elaboration. The causal role of the anopheles mosquito (and hence also of mosquito netting) in the spread of malaria was well known long before the complete etiology of that disease had been worked out. And once again, that role provided useful data for the investi-

25. "Functional Analyses in Biology," *The British Journal for the Philosophy of Science* 17:69-72.

gation. The fact that the notion of cause has this rough-and-ready, intermediate-level usefulness is of enormous practical value to the working scientist. I would argue the same case for functional explanations: establishing one merely indicates the presence of a selection background of some kind and it leaves an enormous amount of theoretical detail completely open. The exact physical mechanism, the precise details of the selection process, in principle even the type of selection (natural or conscious), are not determined merely by establishing a functional ascription-explanation. But, again, establishing such an account provides useful—perhaps essential—data for the further investigation.

The point of these observations is this: because of its characteristic intermediate-level explanatory role, an adequate philosophical analysis of function statement cannot beg these further empirical issues. Any analysis that leans too heavily on details of current evolutionary theory, for instance, is bound to misrepresent one of the most important aspects of function-talk. And this is the most important consideration behind my employment of the normal conversational notion of cause in the analysis offered in this chapter: it is ideally suited to this particular task.

At the end of an analysis that does lean too heavily on explicit detail of underlying theory, Wimsatt remarks

> It may seem paradoxical that attributions of function appear to be better explanations for the origin of the functional trait than an evolutionary narrative which contains far more information. They are not, of course.

But we have already seen a sense in which, of course, they are: they are more certain than any specific underlying account of them because they are consistent with all such accounts. Of course there *are* purposes for which the underlying account is better than the functional one. But this is just what we should expect: they are not rivals. They do different jobs.

DERIVATIVE CASES

There are two kinds of case I wish to discuss under this head, only one of which (the second discussed below) is derivative in the fullest sense: that is, it cannot be accommodated by (F) without modification. A more descriptive characterization of the other category would be 'hybrids.'

Hybrids

These are cases that, although they fit (F), do not do so as distinctly conscious or distinctly natural functions. And since our discussion split across that distinction, it is important to point out the possibility of hybrids on this analysis.

Suppose a primitive tribe were found, the members of which all had what we would call a hip deformity. Suppose also that this deformity, which had the form of a ledge, was used by the members of the tribe to rest a heavy shield (made of locally available material) when battling neighboring tribes; and, further, that a substantial shield was both necessary to have much chance of survival against the weapons available to the neighbors, and too heavy to use without some firm support. If this situation had been relatively stable for a long time we might be able to determine that the selective disadvantage of not having the hip anomaly was so great that the anomaly was actually present in this tribe *because* of its selective advantage in this context. It would be there because it provided support for the heavy shield. Anthropologists would doubtless proclaim in this circumstance that they had discovered the function of the lump; and, of course, (F) would support their judgment. Any hesitancy we might have in this case should be allayed by noticing that most defense mechanisms have to be *used* (claws, spines, sprays, and the like), they do not do their defending by just being there; and many functional defenses involve behavior much more elaborate than shield building: for example, fortifying a home or secluding the young. If, however, we are inclined to suspect the requirement that there be certain kinds of things available locally in order that the lump get a function, we have only to consider the function of protective coloration to rid ourselves of that suspicion.

So here we have a hybrid. The lump gets its function through natural-selective advantage in an evolutionary context, but the advantage is provided, in part, by explicitly conscious effort. The lump would not have the function it does if either aspect were missing. The famous function claims of Dr. Pangloss can be construed as hybrids of this kind; and their fatuity is due to the (obviously) missing etiological component. But the converse of this case, in which we consciously manipulate the environment to produce new strains, is, I think, much less interesting. It can be viewed as natural selection (and hence, can result in natural functions) in an artificially complicated environment. But since environments are simply given in any case, this represents no important difference.

Variants

Under the discussion of 'X does Z,' we concluded that (F)i requires that X at least be *capable* of doing Z, under certain normal conditions. In several contexts, however, we want to be able to say that X has the function Z, even though X can*not* be said to do Z: cases in which X is not even *able* to do Z under the appropriate conditions. A slightly different version of the example considered in the earlier discussion provides an illustration. If the windshield washer switch comes defective from the factory and is never repaired, we would still say that its *function* (italics) is to operate the washer system—which is to say: that is what it is *supposed* to do. Similarly, the *function* of the federal automotive safety regulations is to make driving and riding in a car safer. And this is so even if they actually have just the opposite effect, through some psychodynamic or automotive quirk. Illustrations among natural functions are as easy to find. Pointing to a defective epiglottis, I might say, 'the *function* of that flap is to keep food out of the windpipe, although this one can do nothing of the kind.' This also may be paraphrased: that is what it is *supposed* to do. And this of course points up the fact that we are using 'suppose' here in that famous sense in which 'X is supposed to happen' does not imply that anybody actually supposes X *is* going to happen.

What can we say about such cases? The first thing to notice is that we feel obliged in these cases to italicize (emphasize, underline) the word 'function' in order to make its use plausible and appropriate. This is a logical flag: it signals that a special or peculiar contrast is being made, that the case departs from the paradigms in a systematic but intelligible way. Accordingly, an analysis has to make sense of such a case as a variant. (In fact, an analysis would be suspect if it included them too centrally.) On the present analysis, the italics signals the dropping of the first condition, (F)i: X does *not* result in Z, although, paradoxically, doing Z *is* the reason X is there. And this sounds a bit bizarre until it is recognized that, as we might expect, conscious and natural functions split somewhat further on the variants than they do on the paradigms. For the natural cases, the variation is accommodated by noticing that when talking of an individual case 'X does Z' should be read 'Xs do Z'; and hence the change required is simple: 'Xs *typically* do Z.' So the etiology, the *form* of the explanation is intact, although this instance resembles vestigial cases more than functional ones, and thus is a variant. The conscious cases, in contrast, must be handled somewhat differently. In order to provide a conscious consequence-etiology in terms of Xs resulting in Z, when X does not result in Z, it is necessary to resort to the other sense of 'suppose': *somebody* supposed that X would result in Z, *that's* why it is there. So once again, the etiology is virtually the same as if the thing had worked, it just did not work. And that, of course, is enormously important in the context of functional explanation; so the logic includes an emphatic flag for use at this borderline.

Finally, there are cases of plausibly conscious-functional form which depend on the rich causal possibilities inherent in intent, in conscious contrivance, and which, as far as I can see, have no very close parallels among natural functions. These are cases that, strictly speaking, violate (F)ii, and show the extent to which variant possibilities differ from natural to conscious functions. This, again, is just what we should expect: natural functions represent an extension of only the most center-of-the-page conscious functional case.

As we have seen, first mutations are accidents in the sense relevant here. The first occurrence of a useful physiological structure cannot, on the evolutionary account, be attributed a function: it does not have a consequence-etiology, it did not get there because of what it does. Such structures can be given natural functions only after some consequence of its being where it is becomes part of its etiology and explains how it came to be there. Some conscious function cases are rather like the first mutation case in just this respect, but differ from it in ways that seem to allow the attribution of a function. They must therefore be afforded separate treatment.[26]

Consider the aforementioned engine-oil leak. I discover it to be of sufferable modesty, and withal to keep the grime washed off the timing mark. It functions *as* a timing-mark cleaner, but, so far at least, *has* no function: it is a fortuitous accident. Now it might be the case that I am so taken by the value of this service that, upon having the engine rebuilt, I explicitly instruct the mechanic to restore just that oil drip after he has finished restoring the engine otherwise to normal specifications. This accomplished, I have *given* the oil leak the function of cleaning the timing mark: I have slightly redesigned the engine. And it is now true to say that the leak has a consequence-etiology: it got there because of a consequence of its being there. This case is *not* a variant. In fact it is etiologically similar to the evolutionary case: the useful structure, several generations after it first appeared. The case I am after here, the real variant, is best understood when viewed as a relative of this one.

26. The following represents a major departure from my previously published remarks on functions, especially those in *The Philosophical Review* 82:139-168.

Suppose that the oil leak is serious enough that I would normally have the engine repaired on its account alone, and that there is nothing else wrong with the engine. The tricky case is the one in which I simply decide *not* to repair the engine — not to fix the leak — because the drip cleans the timing mark. It is plausible to argue that at this point I have given the drip the function of cleaning the mark, but it is still not true to say the leak came to be there by virtue of this consequence. So it is important to see how this case differs from a first mutation. It does so by being characterizable subjunctively in a way the first mutation is not, and in a way that assures its status as a variant vis-a-vis (F). If I can justify deciding not to repair the engine by appeal to the cleaning virtue of the oil leak, then, with the same utilities, there are circumstances (of availability, relative cost, and so forth) in which I could justify including the leak in the original *design* of the engine. Hence I can say that, ceteris paribus, the leak *would* be there because of what it did, if it had not gotten there fortuitously. Perhaps we can call this a subjunctive consequence-etiology: the leak does not have a consequence-etiology (and hence strictly violates (F)ii), but ceteris paribus it *would* have a consequence-etiology if it had not occurred fortuitously; so it differs importantly from the first mutation, and in a way that makes it overwhelmingly plausible to include the case as a variant on (F).

CONCLUSION

Extension of the consequence-etiological pattern to cover attributions of function has proven not only possible, but positively enlightening. For in the first place, it meets all the desiderata we have developed in this chapter: it accommodates both conscious and natural functions as functions in the same sense; it makes a cogent function/accident distinction; it accounts for the interchangeability of certain explanatory requests; and it squares with the preanalytic conviction that the functional 'in order to' is a teleological 'in order to.' In addition, it provides an insight into natural selection, shows the relationship between some puzzling peripheral cases and the functional paradigms, displays the possibility of certain hybrid functions—which had not received much attention—and proves that functional explanations are not only respectable, but absolutely required to resolve certain kinds of perplexity.

But perhaps the most important aspect of the argument of this chapter is that it provides further substantial support for the central contention of this essay: the essence of teleology is the consequence-etiology.

CHAPTER IV

EXPLAINING HUMAN ACTION

The preceding analysis casts new light on some of the least tractable problems that arise in the philosophical treatment of human behavior. These problems cluster around the thesis of mechanism, and a defense of one version of that thesis will organize my comments in this chapter. Nearly all the issues that will occupy us here could naturally and appropriately have been treated during our discussion of mechanism in chapter two. They have been grouped together in this place because they tend to be *raised* specifically in the context of human action, and not because their treatment requires considerations systematically different from those marshaled in the earlier section.

We saw in chapter two that there was no reason to suppose that simple teleological behavior could not be the result of, or produced by an underlying, intrinsic, non-teleological mechanism. This, however, leaves open the possibility that certain *kinds* of teleological behavior are, by their very nature, *not* explainable in such terms. Indeed, much of the recent literature on human action has argued that the deliberate behavior of human beings, intentional behavior, is of such a kind: something done "on purpose" can not by its very nature be the result of the interplay of underlying mechanical factors. Several different arguments have been advanced for this view, and will be considered here, seriatim, in a way that leads naturally to a programmatic treatment of the 'other minds' problem based on (T).

[117]

NON-CONTINGENCY[1]

The first of these arguments is a direct sequel to those treated under Mechanism in chapter two. The view that teleological explanations of behavior are essentially dispositional originally arose in the study of *human* behavior: intent, desire, mood, and motive being the fundamental dispositional categories. And it has seemed to some commentators that the very nature of these dispositions disallows the possibility of any kind of mechanism underlying behavior accounted for in terms of these dispositions. For, from this perspective, the fundamental explanatory principle invoked in such explanations is not a contingent proposition, but is rather a matter of logical necessity. And it seems ludicrous to suggest that there could be a mechanism underlying (i.e., offering a further explanation of) a tautology.

The noncontingency of the basic explanatory principle here is developed in this way.

To say that someone wants something is to say that he is disposed to do it or get it . . . that his desiring it issuing in the appropriate action neither requires nor admits of explanations, while the action's not ensuing demands that we adduce some countervailing factor if we are to maintain the claim that he wants the thing concerned.[1]

So, in the absence of countervailing factors, it is *logically impossible to explain* his not doing or getting the thing in question, which means we were wrong to say he wanted it. The same argument applies to the other action-dispositions. Now the antimechanists contend that to ask for an underlying explanation in this case is to ask why the appropriate behavior follows from desire or intent, in the

1. Taylor, *Explanation of Behaviour*, p. 38.

absence of countervailing factors; but from this perspective that is to ask why a tautology is true. So mechanism
seems ruled out on logical grounds.

Although this is still the subject of some controversy,[2] I
take it to be at least plausible to maintain that the connection between wanting or intending to do X and, in the
absence of all countervailing factors, doing X, is one of
logical necessity. If this is mistaken, it is not an important
mistake in this context, and I will accept the proposition
for the following argument. The crucial mistake lies in
the argument *from* this, to the incompatibility of intentional and underlying, mechanistic explanations of
human behavior. The antimechanistic position we are
examining here has, rather naturally I think, usually
been taken to be hostile to the program of current neurophysiology. And although other interpretations are possible, this is the interesting one for our purposes. The
neurophysiologists *are* aiming at a nonteleological
account of what is 'really going on behind human action,'
what is 'really' at the bottom of it. They *are* after 'the
mechanism underlying human behavior.' This in turn
sounds like the sort of account the antimechanist is concerned to rule out.

It is important to make this point explicitly, precisely
because the noncontingency move *fails* to engage the
programmatic claims of the mechanistic neurophysiologists. It is true that they are trying to find an underlying,
mechanistic account of human behavior. The mistake is
in characterizing their activity as an attempt to account
for the fact "that the behavior follows from the intention,
other things being equal." *Of course* they are not

2. See, e.g., J. Thompson, "Comments," *Proceedings of the 7th Inter-American Congress of Philosophy.*

attempting to give a mechanistic account of an action tautology. And accounting for the behavior referred to in the tautology does not require them to. How is this possible?

It is well known that dispositions of a less controversial sort—for example, solubility, brittleness, ferromagnetism, soporific power, and the like—can and do have underlying, structural explanations. We can, for example, offer an explanation of the brittleness of something by appeal, say, to molecular bonding regularities. Furthermore, these bonding regularities *can* be directly appealed to, to explain the fracturing of the object in question (when hit) without explicitly appealing to the brittleness. It is interesting to note what this does *not* show. First, it does not show that there is no brittleness-disposition; the disposition still exists, the object still passes the brittleness tests; we simply have a better understanding of the disposition than we did before. Second, underlying explainability does not show that explanations can no longer be usefully given in terms of the disposition itself: in most contexts in which a dispositional explanation was previously adequate, it will still be adequate; the additional complexity, as before, is irrelevant, and hence antiexplanatory. ("How come you are so fearful of falling?" "My bones have grown brittle in my old age.") Third, exactly the same case can be made for a noncontingent link between brittleness and actual breakage in certain circumstances (proper blow plus absence of countervailing factors) as has been made for action-dispositions. And accepting this characteristic noncontingency in no way discomfits an underlying, structural account of the brittleness. Were there underlying structural regularities they would provide a *contingent* guarantee of the disposition, and hence of the appropriate breakage, in the proper circumstances. But this is consistent with the claim that if the explanation *begins* with the disposition itself, instead of merely a contingent guarantee of it, the explanatory principle is tautological. The proper view of the matter is to see the disposition as a *manifestation of* the underlying regularities. And, sometimes, that we can *count on* the manifestation is all we need to know for an explanation.

Similarly, the fact that dispositions to behave in certain teleological ways play an important role in human behavior is not in the least incompatible with a mechanistic account of that behavior. Accepting the argument of chapter two, the only difference between a teleological disposition and one of the more orthodox variety lies in the convolutedness of the antecedent condition. So the preceding argument applies unmitigated. A mechanistic account of human behavior would, of course, concern itself with the causal antecedents and physiological correlates of action-dispositions, and many others as well: the mechanism should *manifest itself* in those dispositions. Ideally, mechanistic antecedents and correlates would occur in regularities that would provide a contingent, empirical guarantee of the dispositions, and hence provide the same sort of guarantee of the appropriate behavior, in the absence of countervailing factors. But none of this is inconsistent with the claim that *if you start with the dispositions themselves*, rather than merely with a causal guarantee of them, the behavior, in the absence of countervailing factors, follows with logical necessity. Action explanations, that is, explanations in terms of purposes, intentions, desires, and the like, start with the dispositions themselves. Accordingly, the noncontingency argument fails when it is construed as interestingly anti-mechanistic.

NON-CONTINGENCY[II]

There is another sort of noncontingency argument in the
literature, which is sometimes used in conjunction with
the one we have been examining. And although it is perhaps difficult to see how this argument could be understood as an argument against mechanism, it has been so
understood in some places. So it is worth brief consideration here. The clearest statement of the issue is one by
Norman Malcolm, in which he distinguishes between intentions formed prior to the action that is their object,
and other intentions that are not. The former, he allows,
can have an unproblematically causal role in the explanation of human action, but the latter, which he calls
'concurrent simple intentions,' are another story:

> . . .many simple intentions are not formed in advance of the corre-
> sponding action. Driving a car, one suddenly (and intentionally)
> presses the brake pedal: but there was no time before this action
> occurred when one intended to do it. The intention existed only at
> the time of the action, or only *in* the action. Let us call this a merely
> concurrent simple intention. Can an intention of this kind be a
> causal factor in the corresponding action?

> Here we have to remember that if the driver did not press the brake
> intentionally, his pressing of the brake was not unqualified action.
> The presence of simple intention in the action (that is, its being
> intentional) is an analytically necessary condition for its being
> unqualified action. This condition is not a cause but a defining
> condition of unqualified action.[3]

So once again, since the link between the action and its
explanatory principle is not causal, but rather defini-
tional, there cannot be any mechanistic explanation
underlying this one.

3. "The Conceivability of Mechanism," *Philosophical Review* 76:60-61.

Now, although the contrast between defining conditions and causal antecedents has good Humean credentials, it is being abused in this argument. Previously formed simple intentions, to which Malcolm does allow a causal role, have *exactly* the same status as defining conditions of the actions they explain: the behavior in question could not be called action unless it had been brought about by an intention. What defines action here is not the mere presence of an intention. What defines action is that the intention was involved in bringing about the behavior. The causal role of intention is not only consistent with its role in the definition of action, it is *required* by that definition. If we were to use the term 'raccident' to refer to that subset of automobile accidents which were caused by loss of adhesion in the rain, it would be true to say that rain was a defining condition of raccidents. But that would not mean that rain was thereby excluded from playing a causal role in raccidents. For raccidents just are the class of accidents in which rain plays a causal role. And it plays a causal role in *that* class, by definition. Pointing out this fact may help reduce the temptation to misconstrue this uncontentious observation about defining conditions as an argument against mechanism.

It is, however, worth pursuing Malcolm's argument past its implications for mechanism. The above passage contains a basic confusion concerning human action and its explanation, which may be treated with some facility from the perspective of this analysis. Malcolm uses the substantive 'intention' in a way that begs and misrepresents an important explanatory question. He probably saw that something was amiss, which doubtless accounts for the parenthetical identification (of there being an intention with the behavior's being intentional) in the penultimate sentence; but the identification serves merely to point out the problem, and goes no way at all toward resolving it.

The difficulty is most apparent if that identification is taken seriously. If saying there was a concurrent simple intention present in an action is simply equivalent to saying the behavior was intentional, the point of the entire passage suddenly becomes opaque. It then becomes unclear just what the 'analytically necessary condition for unqualified action' amounts to. Who would ever think that its 'being intentional' *might* be the cause of an action, and hence confuse a cause with a defining condition? The answer, of course, is no one. The 'intention' in 'simple concurrent intention' must be construed as a substantive in order that Malcolm's counsel be of any value to us.

On this reading concurrent simple intentions are just like normal, preformed intentions except for the fact that they are not preformed. They do not occur before the action, but they do occur: they are something substantive, something we can pick out and refer to. On this interpretation the point of the passage above is straightforward: we presumably understand the nature of intentions from the standard, paradigmatic cases, and we are simply asked to apply this *familiar* notion in a way we are not accustomed to doing. This construction of the matter, however, misrepresents an important aspect of human action in a number of significant ways.

The problem with the cases Malcolm has in mind is that we usually perform these actions with no reflection whatever. So when asked whether we had any *intention* to do what we did, we are reluctant to give an unqualified affirmation, precisely because this seems to refer to something prior to the action. Nevertheless, we are rightly inclined to say we did it intentionally, because 'intentionally' here contrasts with 'inadvertently,' 'accidentally,' and 'by mistake,' all of which are clearly to be ruled out. The primary job of the adverb is to mark that contrast here. But this way of justifying the use of the adverb in a sentence should lead us to suspect that simple reformulations of the sentence using other forms of 'intend' may not be logically antiseptic; they may not apply to a case in spite of the fact that the adverbial formulation does. Accordingly, if a truism in terms of 'intentionally' seems to become bizarre when formulated in terms of 'intention,' we should be prepared to find that the two formulations actually express different propositions.

Unlike 'intentionally,' all the standard, comfortable cases of the substantive 'intention'[4] are cases in which there is time to mark, express, and perhaps even ponder our intent before the action in question occurs. If there was not even time enough to *note* it, it is strange to say there ever was an intention. Intentions seem to be the sort of thing that *must* be preformed to be effective: if an intention only comes into existence at the time of an action, it certainly was not involved in bringing the action about, and hence cannot brand the behavior 'action' in the usual manner. In the standard cases, the mere existence of an intention to do X does not show that the occurrence of X was an action (I fully intended to have those files destroyed, but they burned with the building before I had a chance to): the intention must share some responsibility for the occurrence of X, in order for X to be an action. So on the substantive reading, simple con-

4. The substantive uses of 'intention' are those which license the claim that the agent *had* an intention to do the thing in question; it is substantive in the sense that it allows a (nonexpletive) pronoun reference: "his intention to go to graduate school dominated his undergraduate study: it structured his curriculum and limited his social life." Of course, there are nonsubstantive uses of the word 'intention' (ones that do not meet the above criteria) to which these remarks do not apply.

current intention seems epiphenomenal. Very likely this paradoxical consequence is what Malcolm was trying to avoid when he inserted, parenthetically, the equivalence-gloss that makes the point of the passage so obscure. There is, however, an easier, more cogent way out.

Normally, when we say that what we did was intentional, *all* we have done is to rule out things like inadvertence, mistake, and accident as accounts of the behavior: several *importantly different* kinds of account of the behavior are still possible. Of course, one sort of alternative account would consist in pointing out that there was an effective intention to do the specific thing in question. But *this* is not the *only* kind of account possible. And the cases Malcolm is concerned with in the above passage are nearly always ones in which a different, more complicated account is required. But before we can see just what sort of account this is, we must sketch in more detail the salient peculiarities of emergency behavior.

Notice that there is something wrong with Malcolm's characterizing this kind of case as *unqualified* action. When we do something of this sort (press the brake, catch the falling vase, duck a punch), when we respond in this way to situations that arise without due warning, much of what we do is over, as we are inclined to say, 'before I had a chance to think.' This importantly differentiates these cases from the paradigm cases of action which are much more clearly deliberate, and hence seems to demand *some* qualification. (It seems least misleading to say that *un*qualified action is action that does result from a pre-formed intention.) Moreover, the word 'reflex' often occurs in descriptions of this kind of action: "Wow! He must have some reflexes to be able to dodge punches like that." And there is something importantly right in this characterization. We often do these things 'automatically,' 'without thinking'; there is some sense in saying we 'couldn't stop ourselves,' ceteris paribus, given the situation. Some would urge that brake-stomping and vase-catching *has* to be automatic if it is to do any good: there often is no time to think. So it is at least misleading to talk of unqualified action here. Still, in most of these cases we want to take credit for *doing* it (pressing the brake, catching the vase, ducking the punch), even though much of what we did can qualify as reflex. But how can we make sense of our calling this kind of quasi-reflex behavior 'action,' without invoking any mythical intention-condensate that materializes as we start to move in an emergency? Quite easily, actually; and the straight-forwardness is only obscured by Malcolm's desperate invocation of simple concurrent intentions to shield these actions against the charge that they are mere reflexes.

The differences between reflex actions, on the one hand, and the standard, center-of-the page cases of reflex such as the knee jerk on the other, are as striking as their similarities. For even though our behavior in these, for example, brake-stomping, vase-catching contexts, is often just as automatic as the knee jerk, it is distinct from knee jerk behavior in two crucial respects. First, the behavior we are disposed to exhibit in these contexts is goal-directed, occurs for the sake of an end. It is characteristic of this behavior that it is, for example, vase-catching behavior, not limb-flailing behavior. We cannot say I (voluntarily) stopped the car or caught the case if one of those things happened while I was randomly flailing my arms and legs. The disposition that gets itself unleashed in these contexts, even if automatically, is a disposition to behave purposively, one that satisfies (T). And goal-directedness is both an important part of action and quite absent from jerk reflexes. Second, this disposition to behave goal-directedly in specific contexts must be something we are personally responsible for: we either developed it ab initio — trained ourselves to behave in that way — or discovered that we naturally behaved in that way and nurtured the disposition against attenuation. A fortiori, these dispositions are ones that we can, perhaps with great effort, change. Through practice, we can get better at braking or ducking punches (though, obviously there are limits). We can even get rid of them: clutch-foot malfeasance after we switch to an automatic. But it is much more central that we have already (before the action) attended to these dispositions, considered them, worked with them, reinforced them, perhaps even created them. In order for punch-ducking to be an action it cannot merely be a flinch reflex: we cannot be incredulous at what we do. So we have an important sort of control over our actions in these reflex action cases, although the control is not immediate, as in the paradigm cases of action, but only over the long haul. This is why these cases are problematic and have to be qualified. But, given normal education and training, it makes perfectly good sense to give credit, and sometimes to hold adults *responsible* for their behavior in these contexts: awareness and control are the only prerequisites.

The the 'other' sort of account intentional behavior can have is this. Even though I never had framed an intention to do just what I did, nevertheless I did it *in order that* some goal be achieved, the behavior was directed toward G, it satisfies (T); and if pressed on the automaticity of my behavior, I produce the story showing I was responsible for that too. This sort of case has all the really salient features of the more paradigmatic sorts of action, so there is nothing very misleading about action-talk on this borderline.

Of course, none of this is to deny that an intention of *some* sort is indirectly involved in bringing about a reflex action. My intention to learn to be a responsible driver is doubtless indirectly causally involved in my stopping my car in an emergency. This is quite consistent with the thesis that I *never* had an intention to stop when and where I did — or even in that particular circumstance (a hotel collapsed on the roadway). It seems best to conclude that the adverbial and nominal forms of 'intend' are related in a very complicated and tenuous fashion here; we can do something intentionally without there ever having been an intention to do it. Certainly this is preferable to the position that some nebulous something bearing so little resemblance to our normal intentions comes mysteriously into existence to accompany the startled movements and sanctify them as action.

RIVALRY

The following argument against the possibility of a mechanism underlying human action is another close relative of one discussed in chapter two. It merits separate treatment largely because it raises some important conceptual issues in a way distinct from the earlier treatment. This argument maintains that since any mechanical explanation underlying allegedly purposive behavior would presumably provide sufficient conditions for the occurrence of that behavior, it follows that the behavior would have occurred, given the mechanical parameters, even if the purposive characterization had been false. Consequently, we would be wrong to invoke purposes in explaining the (occurrence of the) behavior even in the cases in which intentions and purposes are present. Perhaps it is best to let a proponent sketch the argument.

We will recall that the envisaged neurophysiological theory was supposed to provide *sufficient* causal explanations of behavior. Thus the
movements of the man on the ladder would be *completely* accounted
for in terms of electrical, chemical, and mechanical processes in his
body. This would surely imply that his desire or intention to retrieve
his hat had nothing to do with his movement up the ladder. It would
imply that on this same occasion he would have moved up the ladder
in exactly this way even if he had had no intention to retrieve his hat,
or even no intention to climb the ladder. To mention his intention or
purpose would be no explanation, nor even part of an explanation,
of his movements on the ladder. Given the antecedent neurological
states of his bodily system together with general laws correlating
those states with the contractions of muscles and movements of limbs,
he would have moved as he did regardless of his desire or intention. If
every movement of his was completely accounted for by his
antecedent neurophysiological states (his "programming"), then it
was not true that those movements occurred *because* he wanted or
intended to get his hat.[5]

Now the first thing to notice here is that 'it would have
happened anyway' is not an adequate rejoinder to a
causal claim — in spite of its classic credentials. There is
an inexhaustible supply of overdetermination examples —
simultaneous, sequential, linked, or independent — manifesting virtually any logical property we wish, in which
the effect would have happened even if what we rightly
pick out as the cause had not been present. "He would
have died even if the bullet had missed his heart: there
was a cerebral hemorrhage under way at the time." And
although this sort of case might seem completely irrelevant at first, it is not. For these cases show most clearly
that what is important in saying B occurred because of A
is not anything simply formulable in terms of necessary or
sufficient conditions, but rather something much more
complicated. And, accordingly, all that was said in previ-

5. Malcolm, "Conceivability of Mechanism," pp. 52-53.

ous chapters about different levels of explanation, as well as the picture of dispositions as manifestations of underlying structural regularities, cannot be discomfited by anything so facile as "it would have happened anyway."

Furthermore, if we accept the 'manifestation' view of the previous section as the plausible elaboration of the mechanist position, the subjunctive conditional in this objection becomes opaque. It is one of those counterfactuals that really does leave us up in the air. "If Vermont and Georgia were adjacent, then Georgia would be a northern state." It is just not clear. There are an indefinitely large number of geographic changes that would juxtapose Vermont and Georgia. But in only a fraction of those cases would it be accurate to say that Georgia was a northern state: in some it would remain in the South, in others the north/south distinction would be without clear sense. Similarly, suppose we do find a structural state S which manifests itself in a disposition D toward behavior B, and that S together with some other parameters P is sufficient for B. Given just this much it is simply not clear whether S and P would still be sufficient for B if things were such that S no longer manifested itself in D. If we were to change things so radically that S no longer manifested itself in D, what reason do we have to suppose that we would not thereby change the role of S vis-à-vis sufficient conditions for B? A priori there are none, and presumably this objection is not the result of an experiment.

Obviously it is not self-contradictory to say that an S which does not manifest itself in D is, when taken together with P, sufficient for B. But this only shows that B *could* (logically) have happened anyway, not that it *would* (in fact) have happened anyway. And it is the latter claim that is relevant to the explanatory connection in dispute here. What seemed like a truism turns out to be a very difficult and contentious claim indeed. It is like arguing that when you burned your hand on the fireplace poker, it happened not because the poker was hot, but rather because the mean kinetic energy of the poker's particles was very high; for high mean kinetic energy would be sufficient to burn you even if it were not related to high temperature. The mind boggles. Given this much there is simply no reason to prefer the apodosis clause of the counterfactual conditional to its negation. There is no reason to suppose it would have happened anyway.

A more circumspect statement of the argument is given by Charles Taylor:

> . . . if a given piece of behaviour is rightly classified as an action, then we cannot account for it by some *causal antecedent*, where the law linking antecedent (E) to behaviour (B) is not itself conditional on some law or rule governing the intention or purpose. For if the law linking E to B were not dependent on some law linking E and the intention or purpose, I, to do B, then E - B would hold whether or not E - I held. But then B would occur on E whether the corresponding intention was present or not. And then, even when it is present, it cannot be said to bring about the behaviour, so long as this is done by E. Thus to account for B in terms of E would be to offer a rival account, to disqualify B as an action.[6]

This is a particularly interesting statement, because it has misled a number of people who have written on this topic, myself and Taylor among them. If Taylor will allow that the 'manifestation' picture I have sketched above provides an E - B relationship which "is itself conditional on some law or rule governing the intention on purpose," then he has not provided an argument against at least one very plausible form of mechanism: the standard neurophysiological reductionist position escapes his attack. Taylor

6. *Explanation of Behavior*, pp. 34-35.

does say many things, however, both before and after the quoted passage, which makes it pretty clear that he takes any sort of underlying 'programming' regularity to represent an E - B relationship of the offending kind (see especially pp. 20, 40, and 41). But on this interpretation Taylor's argument becomes subject to the same criticism as the less sophisticated formulation; it is merely a complicated way of saying it would have happened anyway. On either reading, Taylor's argument does not succeed against the mechanistic position we have been examining.

Implicit in the last passage from Taylor is a slightly different formulation of this argument, which has found some acceptance in the literature and deserves a brief comment. It is sometimes charged that an underlying structural (e.g., neurophysiological) theory of the sort sketched in the previous section, one which does not make explicit use of the action dispositions themselves, would of necessity govern movements *rather than* action. Hence a theory of that sort could not be called upon to explain action as opposed to behavior which was mere movement. There is just enough cogency in this charge to mislead sanguine commentators into thinking they have made a point against the possibility of mechanism. A neurophysiological theory of the sort envisaged above could well be guilty of this charge when understood in a certain way. For although some of the movements it purports to explain would in fact result from action-dispositions, the theory would not have to distinguish them as such. Behavior resulting from all sorts of dispositions could be lumped together with action in such a theory: for example, subconscious (death wish), unconscious (sleep walking), instinctual (flinch reflex), internal-organic (homeostasis), even hypnotic and pure reflex behavior. For an adequate account of some event in my life, a neurophysi-

ological theory would merely have to produce the physiological parameters in virtue of which I was disposed to
behave in a certain way—and enough else to rule out
countervailing factors. It *could* contain something in its
algorithmic/theoretic details corresponding to 'this is an
action-disposition' (something about consciousness and
goal-directedness), but it need not. From its point of
view, the behavior could occur while I was asleep or
under hypnosis, or it could be reflex. A disposition is a
disposition, a guarantee a guarantee. All the underlying
account requires is that, for example, intent be *inter alia*
a disposition; precisely what the *alia* are does not matter.
But this does not mean that in the context in which the
distinguishing features of these dispositions are interesting, they cannot be distinguished. They can be, and
sometimes should be—underlying explainability once
again notwithstanding. What the underlying theory
explains *are* actions, even if nothing within the theory distinguishes them as such. Just as (part of) what the electro-
magnetic theory of light accounts for *are* individual
colors, although nothing within the theory distinguishes
them as such.

PHYSIOLOGY

The arguments against mechanism considered so far have
been, withal, behavioristic: they have at least been consistent with the view that it is something in the nature of the
behavior itself which determines whether it is action; they
have not found it necessary to appeal to nonbehavioristic
aspects of the 'agent' to prosecute the antimechanistic
thesis. But some antimechanists claim it is precisely this
that cannot be conceded. They argue that since *any* bit of
behavior can (conceivably) be reproduced by a machine,

the nature of the behavior itself can never be sufficient to distinguish conscious, intentional human action from the blind automaticity of an automaton. *Obviously* men are not machines; yet just as obviously Turing was right about the potential dexterity of mechanical devices. So, from this perspective, what licenses my inference to operative mental states — consciousness — in other people is their constitutional or physiological similarity to me. It is *this* sort of similarity, rather than the nature of the behavior, which underwrites action attributions and explanations.[7] It will be interesting to examine this view.

The usual version of this argument might be called the 'whole bodies' version: it bases the inference to other minds on the physiological similarity of entire bodies. "My physiology is very much like yours, therefore, you very likely have active mental states very much like mine." Now it may sound like a typical philosopher's sophistry to ask at the outset "how much is very much?" But it turns out not to be a sophistry at all. For we easily talk of the minds and consciousness of other people whose bodies are different from our own in a large number of ways: just saying something is a person does not guarantee an identical physiology. Furthermore, the differences appear to be significant in this context. There are, for example, the much advertised differences between women and men, and between children and adults. There are the differences between the large group of physiologically normal people on the one hand, and quadruple amputees, Sturge-Weber hemispherectomies, and Thalidomide victims on the other. And there are

---

7. For an interesting, recent defense of this position, see Robert Clack, "Can a Machine be Conscious? — Discussion of Denis Thompson," *The British Journal for the Philosophy of Science* 17:69-72.

artificial—that is, manufactured—bits and pieces: ears,
noses, aortas, trachae, hip sockets and limbs—some of
which are manipulated and articulated directly by the
nervous system. The unweighted catalog of constitutional
bits and pieces can and will vary considerably from person to person, limited, it seems, only by current medical
technology. So, according to the whole-bodies form of
this argument, we should each be able to rank the other
individuals in the human race from 'pretty certainly conscious' through 'unclear' to 'doubtful,' and the latter category should progress toward 'no reason at all to think conscious' with the advance of medicine. Of course, everyone
(everything?) would have is own personal ranking: people
with a substantial number of manufactured parts would
have to rank people with *no* manufactured parts as just as
different from them as machines with *all* manufactured
parts.

My couching this point in terms of the characteristic
'manufactured' might justly elicit some criticism. I have
chosen it primarily because it functions so centrally in the
'minds-and-machines' literature. It might be objected,
for example, that saying something is manufactured is
only to comment on its history, not its physical nature,
and hence this property is illegitimately employed in the
analogical argument. If we could manufacture something that had *all* the constitutional characteristics of me,
all the same purely physical properties, it might be
argued that I would be forced, on the argument from
physiological analogy, to concede that this manufactured
thing is more certainly conscious than my friends who are
physically distinguishable from me. It is important to
raise this point here only to explicitly set it aside as irrelevant. The point I am trying to make can be made as well
using more purely physical properties: people with a sub-

stantial number of plastic parts would have to rank those with no plastic parts as just as different. Either way the picture is a bizarre caricature, not the portrait of reason. The man across the table from me has just returned from Southeast Asia, full of artificial (i.e., manufactured, plastic) pieces and missing essential parts. Yet I still have no reason to doubt his consciousness; there is *nothing* to suggest our conversation is a fraud. And the similarity of our constitutional inventories simply cannot support the weight of this judgment.

It is tempting to try to patch up this argument by moving its focus from the whole body to the brain and central nervous system (CNS) on the grounds of relevance to our mental life. It might seem plausible to argue that the trouble with the whole bodies form of the argument is that, for example, fingernails and tibiae are so palpably irrelevant to our consciousness that to count them at all in the analogical argument is absurd. Furthermore, neurons are not replaceable like hip sockets, so it might appear that the similarities of CNS detail are what should function in this argument. This move has consequences that are every bit as problematic as those of the more straightforward version, but they are logically much more interesting and deserving of attention. They array themselves under four heads.

First, if the antibehaviorist, on the ground of relevance to our mental life, can justify moving from constitutional analogy between whole bodies, to analogy between central nervous systems, he starts down a slippery slope at the bottom of which lurks his anathema: a conscious robot. For the analogical propriety of this move depends essentially upon the potential success of the neurophysiologists in finding a theory of our mental life in terms of observable features of our CNS. The reason for this is as follows.

If such a theory cannot be found, there can be no reason to prefer CNS similarity to whole body similarity in the analogical argument. The functioning of the CNS is crucially dependent upon the rest of our physiology, it cannot get along perfectly well without it: blood must be circulating, lungs functioning, nourishment seeping in. The only justification for saying that our mental life depends on our CNS *as opposed to* our whole body, would have to be based on the contention that particular details of our CNS are relevant to a theoretic understanding of our mental life, whereas particular details of the rest of our physiological makeup are irrelevant to a theoretic understanding of our mental life. For in any other sense, our pleasure and anguish, what we think and dream, depend as much on what is in our stomach or on our toe as they do on what is in our brain or traveling down our neurons. So antibehaviorism here seems to entail mechanism. It even allows the possibility of a conscious robot: If for example, the eventual neurophysiological elaboration of our mental life required by this argument is electrochemical, then robots with the proper distribution of electrochemical activity would be conscious even according to the analogical argument.

Second, since disanalogy infests central nervous systems as well, one of the problems of the whole-bodies version reappears here. We are already familiar with the CNS differences among humans which accompany natural conditions such as right- versus left-handedness, and others that accompany pathological conditions such as brain tumors. Then there are the well-known differences that distinguish quadruplegics and recovered concussion and stroke victims. It is clear from the recovery of stroke victims that there is a great deal of redundancy in the higher levels of the CNS. If some parts of the brain are destroyed, other parts can be made to take over the function previously served by the destroyed part. Furthermore, this redundancy virtually guarantees that, through differences in their learning environment, the brains of normal people will vary somewhat in the distribution of functions. So once again we must concede that we should have profound doubts concerning the consciousness of people who are ordinarily not considered even problematic in this regard. Perhaps more important, it is not at all clear how much doubt goes with how much difference: it is all vaguely reminiscent of the inverted spectrum (How do I know you and I are both having the same "color" *sensation* when we are both seeing a yellow patch?).

Third, until relatively recent neurophysiological investigation, similarities of the sort required by the CNS analogical argument could not be made sense of easily. In the absence of neurophysiological detail, all that could have supported CNS analogy was some feeble historical-ontogenetic data, together perhaps with some crude speculation about disabling injuries; and it might be considered stretching the point to view that as a version of the same argument. In any case, from this perspective, Aristotle and his contemporaries should have had much more profound doubts about each other's consciousness than we, and much more than records suggest they did. Our prehistoric ancestors should have had even deeper reservations. And, of course, these points apply respectively to people today who have the physiological sophistication of Greeks or cavemen. If we accept the CNS analogical position, we must concede that only a minute, physiologically sophisticated fraction of the human race—and nobody until quite recently—has ever had good reason to think anyone else had operative mental states.

The fourth interesting consequence of this position develops out of the third. It seems conceivable — easily imaginable, if you have a mind for science fiction — that the history of neurophysiology has been very different from what it was. Surely it could (logically possibly) have been discovered that the physiological center of mental life varied in location, chemical constitution, appearance, and the like, from individual to individual. In this case, however, reasoning by analogy, we should have enormously increased doubts concerning the consciousness of other people: the analogical argument is conclusively negative in this eventuality. To discover the individual variability of the physiological locus and nature of mental life is to eliminate the only reason we have to suppose other people *have* a mental life on this argument. On this view, such a discovery *would* be logically impossible. In fact, if our inference to other minds depends crucially upon our knowledge of analogous features of nervous systems, then basic neurophysiology should proceed in a way very different from the way it does. The only legitimate method would require the neuroscientist to become intimately familiar first with the operation of his *own* CNS, before he is in a position to sensibly investigate the physiological roots of consciousness in others. Of course, the logical and methodological consequences of this requirement would make neuroscience a much more difficult and parochial endeavor than it is under the present dispensation. But it is perhaps more significant that the practical difficulties of this requirement would make neuroscience virtually impossible. It is not at all clear that I *could* adequately investigate my own CNS without disabling it in a way that would prevent the investigation from proceeding.

In sum, the CNS analogical position entails that current neurophysiology is radically misguided, both in theoretic structure and procedure; that virtually no one has ever in fact had good reason to believe anyone else to have operative mental states; that there is a general-but-unrecognized logical/conceptual shoddiness in the use of mental language, which is, however, seemingly unproblematic in the usual contexts; that the inference to other minds has the logical structure of the discredited inverted spectrum inference; and withal it still allows the possibility of a conscious robot. Surely, to accept all this for the sake of maintaining the analogical argument is to save a theory at the expense of everything it was supposed to account for. Each of these paradoxical consequences *individually* provides good reason to seek a view of mental concepts which accounts differently and better for our knowledge of other minds. *Together* they provide a truly awesome barrier to representing the structure of mental discourse in the way required by the physioanalogical position. Fortunately, there is an alternative waiting in the wings.

Our practically universal failure to allocate doubt about the consciousness of others in proportion to our knowledge of their analogous and disanalogous physiological features need not be attributed to widespread logical obtuseness. On the contrary, it is probably due to the tacit recognition that an argument from analogy cannot possibly carry any weight in this context. Analogy here is as worthless as it is in the inverted spectrum puzzle. There simply is no way to discover how much alike two things must be to justify an inference to these "internal" similarities. There is no way to decide whether the difference in constitutional similarity between me and another human on the one hand, and me and a machine on the other, is of a magnitude important to the distinction between good and bad reasons for an inference to consciousness. A fortiori, we cannot argue that this difference outweighs — or even rivals — similarities in behavior patterns. Details of behavior are, after all, what is being *explained* by appeal to the quasi-theoretical terms of mental life, so *they* are *clearly* relevant. Nobody even entertains the denial of that.

Furthermore, giving behavior the position of primacy here accords well with the history of neurophysiology which raised such enormous difficulties for the analogical argument. For it was through the study of *behavior* that we discovered that there *is* a central nervous system. It was only through observation of behavior that we discovered that the brain, as opposed to the heart or liver, plays a central physiological role in our mental life. For the neurophysiologist, just like everybody else, the touchstone is behavior.

To suppose that everyone from scientists to our ancestors have been using an entire conceptual framework in a systematic and coherent way without ever having at their disposal the only features of the world which would allow them to do so, is not only the apotheosis of analytical arrogance, it is simply incredible. And if the sole motivation for taking this bizarre and implausible position is that it clearly separates the men from the machines, then, as we have seen, the motivation is mythical: the last vestige of support has vanished.

It was not any physiological discovery that convinced the police chief of that small Southern town that Negro Virgil Tibbs was 'just like us.' It was Tibb's *behavior*: his passion, his commitment, his rhetoric. For the chief, Negroes were as much unlike him as something inorganic. He might well have reacted in the same way had Virgil Tibbs been a metallic dull grey.

INTENTIONAL PROPERTIES:
THE PERSPECTIVE OF AN AGENT

In the ascription of consciousness, the role of analogy is the same as it is in the ascription of the (merely) goal-directed behavior of animals and mechanisms. Analogy with what I might do, feel or think in a given situation may explain my *insight*: it may explain how I ever thought of explaining the behavior of something else in terms of mental life; but it does not constitute a justification for explaining it that way. The *justification* must consist in showing that the ascription of some details of mental life is demanded by the behavior patterns in question. But what is it for behavior patterns to demand the ascription of a mental life, of consciousness, of intentional properties? What is the distinction between a heuristic and an explanation here? From the vantage provided by the present analysis this question, remarkably enough, has a clear answer. For on this analysis, that question is just a specific version of a much more general one: what is it for any phenomenon to demand a particular causal or theoretical account? And we know what counts as an answer to that. At a certain point in the investigation the conclusion is clear: the crash was caused by a broken hub carrier, the data demand that account of the matter. In more mundane cases we need no investigation: the noise was caused by the shotgun discharge, the pain by the punch. Dispositional and theoretical cases are closer to the point: the bone broke because it was extremely brittle (the data demand that conclusion), and the brittleness was due to osteoporosis. Its low melting point caused the wax figure to distort in the sun; there is simply no question about it. But, one still might ask, how is this like an inference to mental life?

With very slight modifications, the same things may be said about the perspectives of human agents as was claimed for those of nonhuman "agents" in chapter two. For this demonstration we must rely on one-man objectivity tests, but this raises no important logical issues: it was possible for Robinson Crusoe to do objective physics even before Friday. We can apply (T) to the behavior of men as well as mice. We can demonstrate (justify) in the same way that a bit of behavior has a consequence-etiology. But on the lower levels of performance, nothing demands a mental life: we cannot by inspection distinguish conscious from subconscious from reflex behavior there. Mental terms are forced on us only as a way of characterizing in an intelligible way the incredible complexity of the (largely teleological) dispositional state of affairs that manifests itself in typical human behavior. The rudiments were present earlier in the objective propriety judgments involved in applying (T) to certain kinds of unsuccessful animate behavior. But those cases scarcely exercise our perceptual apparatus; we are able to detect variations in behavior due not only to much subtler misperceptions than those discussed there but also to the changing weight of competing goals. Even for animals, we can often justify such things as, "He has just noticed (i.e., seen) the bird on the fence" or, "There is some ambivalence, it clearly wants the food, but is afraid to come too close to us." And we can do so by simple extension of the procedure discussed in chapter two. The former is a special sort of activation phenomenon concerned specifically with sensory reception: suddenly, and in a characteristic manner, (T) becomes relevant to the behavior in a new way, and a new G is substituted. The latter involves conflicting teleological dispositions. The distortion of the behavior vis-à-vis normal behavior

directed at either goal independently is due to the
attempt to satisfy the propriety criteria for both simultaneously — which ex hypothesi is very difficult. 'Hesita-
tion' characterizes a kind of distortion under this head.
The behavior occurs because it tends to produce both G_1
and G_2; but saying that these goals conflict is saying that
behavior at the very extreme of propriety is required for
one or the other or both. Relative strength of the goals is
determinable if we can roughly estimate a 'degree of
extremity' within the range of appropriate behavior for
each. In artificially contrived circumstances, such as
those described earlier, we can get all sorts of rather
straightforward evidence for these claims: independent
tests of perceptions, directionality of perceptors, standard
reaction (patterns) to birds, or, alternatively, eating
ritual, standard reaction to 'us,' and variability of behavior with 'our' distance from the food. But, of course, each
of these tests, as is always the case in any evidence-gather-
ing activity, consists in finding the best account (explanation) of an observed phenomenon; and this is also true of
our objective attributions of perceptions and other
mental-life phenomena in ordinary (nontest) circumstances. The major difference between test cases and less
artificially contrived circumstances is merely that we are
able to bring more data directly to bear on a single bit of
behavior in the test cases; it is definitely *not* that we are
legitimately always more certain in those cases. For what
the more pedestrian case lacks in experimental richness,
it can make up for in long-term familiarity and in perceptions trained to a specific, parochial context. "Nothing
can tear her away from a good scratching like a bird
lighting on that fence: as soon as she spots one, off she
goes, upper lip twitching atavistically away."

It is clear in such cases that the impact of seeing and

desiring on behavior is indeed dispositional in the way the antimechanists contend, and the account of the behavior in those terms must reflect that fact. We could, clearly, restrain or distract the animal when it spots the bird, the food or the predator. All the seeing and the wanting tell us is what the animal is disposed to do, ceteris paribus; and the 'do' here is that peculiar 'do' that invokes (T): what it is disposed to do is goal-directed. Conflicting teleological dispositions are worked out in principle in just the same way as conflicting tendencies of a body to behave in a complex force-field are worked out in mechanics. We often infer the shape of the force-field from what the body does, just as we infer desires and perceptions from animate and human behavior. Obviously, only *some* of the constraints on animate behavior will be competing teleodispositions: some will be mechanical or physiological limitations. The force-field simile accommodates this too: only some of the constraints on the pith ball are electrostatic; at the macrolevel, solid walls and surfaces represent a different *kind* of limit.[8]

The major difference between merely animate cases and humans is that through linguistic articulation, through conversation, there is vastly more data available in the case of humans, and hence it is possible to provide objective fine-structure to the mental apparatus account for humans which is simply beyond justification in typical animals.[9] When we talk of what someone else thinks, or

8. Although there are some important disanalogies, agency, on this model, is like the charge on the body; a great deal of the complexity of animate behavior is due to the variability of reactions to the same conditions, and this can be represented as a variability of charge on the body, So whether or not the variation of charge on a single body is a discoverable function of time represents the predictability version of the free-will problem.

9. But note that people who have never had pets have trouble conceiving of even the amount of fine-structure pet owners attribute to animals. This is probably due to the

hopes, or sees, or wants, or remembers, we are most importantly trying to place certain aspects of the dispositional context into the categories of a conceptual framework that we have found useful in understanding human behavior. The salient distinguishing feature of these dispositions is that they are teleological, that they conform to (T).

If the mental life picture is appropriate — that is, if the behavior is intentional — and if we have the dispositional categories assessed properly, then attributing mental life to an individual allows us to understand his behavior. And that understanding is testable in the standard way: successful prediction of future behavior (including verbal behavior) and an ability to account for unpredicted behavior consistently with that picture without implausibly ad hoc suppositions. Of course, the clearest *isolated* bits of data consist in performance under "test" conditions: response to pointed questions, or to proffered opportunity. But even the evidential value of these tests relies heavily on our irreducible perceptual grasp of the dispositional context: is this a context in which he is likely to lie? to be modest? to repress his real desire? The categories of mendacity, modesty, and repression are highly dispositional in character. And they are typical of the kinds of category included in the conceptual framework mere mortals require in order to have reliable perceptions of the enormously complex phenomena of human behavior. So the ultimate test of our perceptual reliability is our ability to prosecute sustained analyses of human behavior in these terms without encountering a succession of intractable absurdities. This in turn is the ultimate evi-

widespread human tendency to be prudently skeptical of the reliability of a subtle perceptual skill until one possesses it himself.

dence for the general propriety of the mental life picture: reliable perceptions are the best evidence that there is something to perceive. So the 'isolated' bits are not really isolated, they are part of the bigger picture and are worthless apart from it. But they are striking, and legitimately so, because they mark issues on which the perceptual categories are clear and boldly drawn, and hence are areas in which our perceptions are most acute. ("I can usually tell when a witness is lying," or "Nothing is more obvious than false modesty," or "He's so transparently repressing his concern that it's embarrassing.")

Further, insofar as an agent's perception—his perspective—is relevant to explaining his action, exactly the same considerations hold. For insofar as they are relevant to explaining his action, an agent's perceptions may be assimilated into what he thinks, what he believes to be the case. And *this* can be given a sufficiently dispositional interpretation to fit the above formulation. Very often—though not always—we can *tell* what somebody sees or thinks (or thinks he sees) from what he is disposed to do or say, even if the agent would rather not have us know. We can even correct his own impression of his perceptions and beliefs, as happens frequently in ordinary psychotherapeutic exercises.

We may show that much of what men think of their own behavior is not only untrue, but the result of a powerful drive towards self-deception or repression. But this is to appeal from how men say that they see their situation to how they really see it; it is not to make this dimension irrelevant. From this point of view, therefore, psychoanalysis is a development of explanation by purpose. For recognizing that much thought and motivation is unconscious, it accounts for this in terms of goals; indeed, repression itself is accounted for teleologically; and thus a central aspect of psychoanalytic explanation concerns the meanings that events, situations, symbols, have for the agent, even if these are unconscious.[10]

To say this, of course, is not to say everything about perceptions, and very little about the epistemology of perception. But it is to say enough about the subject to show that an agent's perspective raises no logical difficulties for the picture of action explanations I am painting here. Furthermore, as far as I can see, none of this entails that, for example, beliefs *are* dispositions. All it requires is that the impact of beliefs (etc.) on action can be characterized in a dispositional way. And this is less contentious.[11]

The understanding gained from placing certain aspects of human behavior in these very complex dispositional categories of mental life is importantly like what we gain from placing certain aspects of dynamic phenomena into the categories of Newtonian mechanics: thinking of the behavior of inert bodies in terms of mass-centers, moments of inertia, and the laws of motion serves in the same way to make a complex and chaotic phenomenon

10. From C. Taylor, "The Explanation of Purposive Behavior," in *Explanation in the Behavioural Sciences,* ed. R. Borger and F. Cioffi (Cambridge: Cambridge University Press, 1970), p. 60.

11. It is probably worth mentioning in this connection that what seems to be the most current of the arguments alleged to show that mental notions such as desire, intent, and belief *cannot* be dispositions is not cogent. This is the argument that such a conclusion follows from the fact that we can know what we desire, intend, believe, etc., without inferring from our own behavior that we are disposed to behave in the way appropriate to that desire, intention, and the rest. But surely action-dispositions, just like solubility and brittleness, can have regular correlates that we can come to recognize; and these can be used to detect the presence of those dispositions even in the complete absence of any manifest behavior. Just as we can tell from the look of something that it is glass, and hence brittle, or from the taste that it is sugar and hence soluble in water, we can tell by the feel that we have a desire, and often what the desire is a desire for. And, of course, there doesn't even have to be any 'feeling': the correlate may simply be a reliable judgment of the state. The state still could *be* a disposition, and the reliability of the judgment empirically testable. This also accords well with the above passage from Charles Taylor: it is possible for first-person judgments to be mistaken about such matters.

intelligible. It does not matter in the least that our perceptual competence in the former case involves empathy
which, of course, it need not always do. What matters,
again, is that we can account for human behavior in this
manner without implausible, ad hoc additions and modifications; and this is just as true of the mechanics of inert
bodies. The methodological principles necessary to apply
(T) to even very complex behavior are all pretty well
understood, and are sketched in chapter two. This provides the *framework* for checking our complex, empathic
perceptual diagnoses of mental state configurations. It
may *occur* to me to explain something else's behavior in
terms of mental life only because *I* have a mental life and
it does something I might well (consciously) do. That
nevertheless does not *justify* the explanation (and hence
the attribution of a mental life). The justification has got
to be that the behavior is appropriately baroque from the
teleodispositional point of view: it has to *require* all the
subjunctive possibilities inherent in the conscious entertaining of ends-in-view and, for example, in changing
one's mind. True, less complex behavior on the part of a
missile — or even a rock — *could* (logically possibly) be con-

---

Of course there are other, very strong objections to saying that all of the major substantive terms of mental life simply stand for dispositions. The most reasonable position at this stage seems to be that some are simply dispositions (moods, e.g., and perhaps desires), while others are not (images and sensations, e.g., and perhaps
thoughts). But while some of the features of normal, human mental life are *not* simply
dispositions, it is crucial to notice that our logical and empirical access to these features is solely through the dispositions that are their natural manifestations. There is a
strict, logical link between mental states and what they dispose us to do; it is only because of this that mental states can explain and help us understand our behavior. Pain
is *whatever* it is that causes me to react in a certain characteristic manner: that is how *I*
found out what 'thing' is called 'pain.' Originally, I was told when I was in pain, by
people observing what I was disposed to do. All I had to know was that *something* was
making me writhe and cry — I was not working at it — 'they' told me what it was, no
matter *what* it was. Other kinds of mental phenomena are more complicated because
of their dispositional interdependency.

scious, result from mental states. But we know from our experience with missiles and rocks that this is immensely implausible. The hip *could* have been broken before the fall and been held together by an imperceptible spider web which was instantaneously dismantled coincidentally with the thump. It is just stupendously implausible, not a serious possibility, nothing we should waste our time thinking about. Conversation, of course, provides a great deal of the data necessary to justify (demand) mental-life attributions; but there is enough richness in body movements and facial expression for cats to have character.

If mental state categories are primarily ways of getting a systematic handle on an enormously complicated dispositional context, then the scientific objectivity of mental state discourse raises no special methodological problems. The rules are generable from solubility and brittleness tests merely by recursive application of (T). And there should be no more difficulty imagining a neurophysiological mechanism underlying human behavior than there is imagining bonding regularities underlying the impact-behavior of glass.

Once again, as in chapter two, it is worth pointing out that none of this is inconsistent with the fact that there are numerous occasions in which there is no objective, external way to determine the mental states crucially relevant to the explanation of a bit of behavior — no way to discover the agent's perspective. These are simply cases in which there is no objective way to provide an account of the behavior. Any theory, any type of explanation, faces possibilities like this. All that the scientific objectivity of mental states requires is that there be instances in which the dispositional fine-structure *is* objectively determinable; that is enough to give ordinary action explanations all the empirical credentials they need.

INDEX